ROUTLEDGE LIBRARY
ENGLISH CIVIL

Volume 4

ATLAS OF THE
ENGLISH CIVIL WAR

ATLAS OF THE
ENGLISH CIVIL WAR

PETER NEWMAN

Routledge
Taylor & Francis Group

LONDON AND NEW YORK

First published in 1985 by Croom Helm.

This edition first published in 2021
by Routledge
2 Park Square, Milton Park, Abingdon, Oxon OX14 4RN

and by Routledge
52 Vanderbilt Avenue, New York, NY 10017

Routledge is an imprint of the Taylor & Francis Group, an informa business

© 1985 P. R. Newman

British Library Cataloguing in Publication Data
A catalogue record for this book is available from the British Library

ISBN: 978-0-367-60972-6 (Set)
ISBN: 978-1-00-310733-0 (Set) (ebk)
ISBN: 978-0-367-61670-0 (Volume 4) (hbk)
ISBN: 978-0-367-61674-8 (Volume 4) (pbk)
ISBN: 978-1-00-310595-4 (Volume 4) (ebk)

Publisher's Note
The publisher has gone to great lengths to ensure the quality of this reprint but points out that some imperfections in the original copies may be apparent.

Disclaimer
The publisher has made every effort to trace copyright holders and would welcome correspondence from those they have been unable to trace.

ATLAS OF THE ENGLISH CIVIL WAR

PETER NEWMAN

CROOM HELM
London & Sydney

© 1985 P.R. Newman
Croom Helm Ltd, Provident House, Burrell Row,
Beckenham, Kent BR3 1AT

Croom Helm Australia, First Floor, 139 King Street,
Sydney, NSW 2001, Australia

British Library Cataloguing in Publication Data

Newman, Peter
  Atlas of the English Civil War.
  1. Great Britain——History——Civil War,
  1642–1649——Maps.
  I. Title
  911'.42   G181.21.S/

  ISBN 0–7099–1811–9

Printed and bound in Great Britain

CONTENTS

INTRODUCTION

This book is concerned with the topography of the English Civil Wars of 1642–51 and, to a lesser extent, with events prior and subsequent to those dates. It sets out to fill a gap in the available literature concerning the period, by offering a series of complementary texts and maps aimed at explaining, for the most part, the sometimes confusing prose accounts of campaigns and battles. Over the last thirty years or so, there has been a marked and widespread interest in the civil wars amongst a more general readership, an interest to some extent created and satisfied by 'military histories', of varying quality, of the civil wars. The best of these, those of Burne and Young (1959), Woolrych (1961) and Young and Holmes (1974), have presented first-class accounts of specific campaigns and battles linked together with brief, explanatory texts. The worst have sought to encompass everything, touching lightly and inadequately upon social, political, economic and religious causes of the civil wars as a means of putting military events 'in context'.

Such an approach was only possible when the issues, even to historians of stature such as Gardiner or Firth, appeared more clear cut than they actually were. No single book can hope to encompass with any balance every aspect of the years 1642–51, let alone the years leading up to civil war and the events subsequent upon the fall of the monarchy. Few, if any, professional historians would have the temerity to suppose themselves capable of producing such a study. Historical research, if it is to contribute properly to our general understanding of the past, has become and will remain an area of relatively narrow specialisation. The general readership of books dealing with the civil war will, therefore, be better served by books setting out a specific theme or adopting a clear approach.

This atlas can be used, it is hoped, both in its own right as a source for understanding the military developments from 1642 onwards, charting the progress by which the King lost, and the Parliament won, the war; and also as an adjunct to more detailed military histories as well as other works which touch in passing upon military events. It is, in other words, an aid to understanding, and does not pretend to offer any original insight into events themselves, except where account has been taken of pertinent advances in scholarship to explain events or phenomena; for example, the appearance of the Clubmen and the unrest in the New Model Army.

The value of maps in dealing with military campaigns will be self-evident. Not only do they elucidate occasionally confusing written accounts, but they also serve to provide the general reader with a spatial context for events. They offer an opportunity to trace the progress of war both in specific regions and localities, as well as provide a broader picture of those areas of the country which saw much, and those which saw little, prolonged fighting. They show, for example, that whereas the whole of the country was involved in one way or another in the war effort of either side (and sometimes both, depending upon which had the upper hand), not everywhere saw fighting, either on a large or a small scale. Kent, for example, remained virtually untroubled, at least until 1648, and the same was true of Essex; whilst counties like Cumberland and Westmorland, ostensibly royalist in outlook and alignment, experienced little or no real action until late in 1644, whereas Lancashire to their south had been fought over quite extensively in 1642/3 and early 1644. The Midlands, the south-west and the Welsh border lands were the major battlegrounds of the civil war years 1642–6. It will also be apparent that military objectives were hardly ever conceived on a grand scale. The King's march on London in late 1642 after Edgehill was an obvious step for him to take, but it came to nothing when London faced up to his army at Turnham Green in November. Thereafter, no general strategy aimed at the reduction of the capital was promulgated in the royalist high command, unless the alleged triple advance on the city in late 1643 involving the royalist northern army as a major element had any grounding in fact, which is doubtful. Objectives were limited: the capture of a city here, a fortified place there, and the occasional but largely unproductive major battle (Marston Moor and Naseby, both victories for the Parliament, were exceptions to this) punctuating wars of manoeuvre, march and counter-march, and intermittent but bloody skirmishing and raiding. Both sides were also subject to the concept of the 'campaign season', and the relative inactivity of wintertime. Indeed, the Scottish invasion in January 1644 may have been launched to try to take advantage of the royalist northern army lying in winter-quarters, but if so, it was only partially successful, since the royalists rapidly responded.

Civil War England

Civil War England, topographically and in many other senses too, was thoroughly different from the England of the nineteenth and twentieth centuries. It presented, in reality, a series of major obstacles to successful military campaigning, in the nature of its countryside, its road system and its means of communication. Even synchronisation of events on the battlefield was virtually impossible, although some officers possessed pocket watches and some had telescopes (perspective glasses). If history is nothing more than a catalogue of errors and miscalculations, as some believe, then the period of the civil wars in many respects, including the military one, was a case in point. The royalists lost the battle of Marston Moor.in July 1644 largely because Prince Rupert miscalculated as to what his opponents would do, and because one of his sub-ordinates made a fatal error in disobeying orders as battle commenced. The parliamentary New Model Army almost lost the battle of Naseby in June 1645 because they imagined victory would be an easy task. Once a general had committed his forces to action, the successful outcome of that engagement might very well turn upon decisions taken in isolation on the field by regimental or company and troop commanders. The secret of good generalship then, as now, lay in being able to foresee the limi-

tations of plans and in being able to capitalise upon mistakes made by the enemy. Cromwell, at Marston Moor and at Naseby, showed himself to be a good general in the field because of this. In other aspects of the period, too, the same human capacity for folly revealed itself. King Charles I, in 1647 and in 1648, chose to suppose that he could indefinitely deceive and lie to his enemies, and made his way to the block in 1649 as a consequence. The exiled royalists in the 1650s seriously believed, or some of them did, that the Republic could be overthrown by conspiracy and plot, the only outcome of which was to add further names to the lists of royalist martyrs in enterprises doomed from their inception. Thus, in dealing with the military events of 1642–51, it has to be understood that 'strategy' and 'tactics' were as often as not improvised, that no broad or coherent plans as such were ever seriously contemplated or followed through, beyond the resolution of either side that it should win the war: even that resolution was something that was not wholeheartedly endorsed by all the leaders of both sides.

The England of 1642 was a rural country reliant upon agriculture for its wealth, with trade primarily involved in the distribution of agricultural produce both internally and overseas. There were certain major cities, London far and away the largest and the richest, being the centre of the country's financial life, but none on any scale to compare with what would today be recognised as substantial. Most people lived in the countryside, in townships of varying size, or in hamlets and isolated farmsteads, these latter tending to predominate in the pastoral areas of north-western and western England and Wales. Parts of the North-East, the whole of the Midlands and East Anglia, were areas of mixed farming, corn-growing and animal husbandry, and although within this latter region there were areas of enclosure, of hedged and fenced fields held in severalty, it was for the most part composed of open, common fields with large tracts of waste land known as commons or moors. This type of landscape might offer suitable ground for the movement of armies, but it also offered little or no cover. There were still extensive forest regions to be met with, although not all forests were extensively planted with trees, despite the processes of disafforestation which had been going on for centuries. In the north were the great forests of Pickering and Galtres in Yorkshire, and Delamere in Cheshire. In the North Midlands were the forests of Macclesfield, Needwood, Cannock, Sherwood and Charnwood. Further south in the Midlands lay Leicester Forest and those of Rutland, Rockingham, Salcey and Whittlewood, Kinver, Feckenham, the Forest of Arden and the Forest of Dean. The Forest of Dean contained the only substantial deposits of iron ore that the royalists were able to keep for a time in their power, hence the importance to Parliament of its garrison in Gloucester which managed on the whole to restrict royalist activity in the Forest.

The forests, however, presented no major obstacle to the movement of men and supplies, as they had presented no real obstacle to the progressive colonisation of the land in previous centuries. The arteries of the Kingdom were its roads and waterways, and it was upon their capacity to facilitate movement of large bodies of men that much campaigning turned. Most roads, even the major routes, were in fact appalling, there being no single authority responsible for their overall condition. Each township through which a road passed bore responsibility for its upkeep within the township's territory, and lack of resources or indifference often meant that most roads were virtually impassable in winter rain, and rutted and difficult in summertime. Perhaps because of road conditions, means of transport were limited. Wagons and carts were not common everywhere: in Cornwall, for example, wheeled vehicles were scarcely seen, and the same was true of large parts of Yorkshire and of the West of England generally. Most carriage was by packhorse team, and most people, if they could not afford horses, rode very rarely, travelling mostly on foot. Sledges at all seasons of the year were not unusual, and carts on revolving axles and often two-wheeled were about the best most parts of the country could afford. Many roads were seriously neglected in favour of narrow, stone-based tracks alongside them, 'pack and prime ways' to facilitate the movement of teams of packhorses. The nearer to London and to the Home Counties, the more likely the traveller would be to find wagons and coaches, but in most of England over which the civil wars were fought, transport was hideously difficult and restricted. Many complaints made of horses being plundered from their owners by armies on the move suggest that horses were not only seized for cavalry mounts, but also to provide means of carriage. Some heavy cannon, for example, the demi-culverin and culverin, required

teams of seven and eight horses respectively to pull them, equivalent to between 40 and 50 men. The common sense of having campaigning seasons restricted to months when good weather could be anticipated is clear. Armies moved slowly anyway, and in winter they might not move at all, at least, not in any large numbers, or if they did so, might be so strung out across the countryside as to lose all order of march. In open-field England, moreover, roads or trackways were by no means fixed and constant features of the terrain; they shifted as cropping practices dictated in whichever rotation, two, three or four field, was followed in a given area. It was quite normal, where roads did exist as a fixed feature, for travellers even in times of peace to spread themselves a hundred yards or more either side of a route to try to find firmer going, trampling crops underfoot and presumably getting away with it. Armies on the move would do this with impunity, and they would also not infrequently steal the crops in the fields if the season was right. Thus England was a country where the major roads were defined but often impassable in places, and where the minor tracks were as often as not equally as treacherous and by no means fixed.

The Nature of Armies

It used to be maintained that the rough division of the country which prevailed after civil war began, the parliamentarian zone of the South and South-East and East against the royalist zone of the North, Wales and the West, corresponded to areas of allegiance. That is to say, that the backward, pastoral regions supported the King, and the more forward-looking eastern areas, Parliament. In fact, whilst it is true that the King began his war with recruitment in the North-East and in the Welsh border areas, and Parliament likewise in London and the Home Counties, this division of the country was a consequence of campaigns in 1642 and the King's failure to take London in that year. If the old view of allegiance had had any merit, then Lancashire, Cheshire and Yorkshire, for example, would not have seen such heavy fighting as they did see in 1643/4, evidence of the very real split within the county communities. Allegiance did not follow any geographical divisions, and although Kent remained firmly parliamentarian because of the proximity of London, dozens of Kentish gentlemen and others abandoned their county and served the King elsewhere. Similarly, Norfolk and Suffolk were not so firmly parliamentarian because of their geographical location, but because what gentry there was in those counties tended to be for the Parliament. Their outnumbered royalist neighbours either kept quiet or quit the counties, rather as parliamentarian gentry fled from areas under royalist domination. The civil war split the country deeply, and all areas provided men for both armies at one time or another. The campaigning regions of the Midlands and South-West produced forces and supporters for both sides, and if the numbers of men available to the King declined as the war went on and the royalist cause suffered reverses, nevertheless some kind of balance was maintained by the overall quality of the royalist commanders in the field who, man for man, were probably better at their jobs than their opponents. Parliament fought the King to a standstill, it needs to be remembered, and did not overwhelm him in the field: but there were other factors involved in that victory, not least parliamentary access to money supplies in London and the reorganisation of Parliament's armies resulting in the New Model of 1645. It has also recently been argued that Prince Rupert did much to undermine the royalist war effort from 1644 onwards, and materially contributed to the King's defeat. Whatever validity that view may have, it serves to demonstrate that the King's defeat is still a matter for argument, the precise reasons for his failure not yet having been clearly defined. The first civil war lasted four years, and that it lasted so long must be taken as evidence of the widespread support that both sides enjoyed. It was never a case of an unpopular royalist faction trying to overcome a populist parliamentarian movement, for if it had been, the war would have gone against the King at the outset.

The King, after all, had no army to call upon instantly in 1642, nor, apart from forces readied for Ireland, did the Parliament. England possessed no standing army as such, nor had it traditionally maintained one. Apart from the monstrous expense of such an undertaking, there was no real need for it. Foreign mercenaries had been employed when necessary in the sixteenth century, particularly during the troubles with Scotland in the reign of Edward VI, and were used against rebels in East Anglia and the West Country in 1549. Foreign mercenaries had proved almost as unpopular as the native-born soldiery, and there

was a general reluctance on the part of most of the English people to involve themselves in military matters. Nevertheless, in a country where no army existed, two emerged in the course of 1642 and developed into fairly formidable fighting forces during the course of 1643. That of the royalists disappeared entirely in 1646, but that of Parliament survived attempts to disband it after victory was won, and became the arbiter of political matters from 1648 onwards. Where did these armies come from? Although perhaps it should not be stressed, recent research has tried to suggest that the King's army at least was composed of Irishmen and officered by mercenaries and a few gentlemen and noblemen. That is an historical nonsense. The civil war was just that, a 'civil war', fought between Englishmen and Welshmen, with occasional help from Irishmen and Scotsmen and a mere sprinkling of European mercenary officers and rank and file, on both sides. There were enough native-born English and Welsh prepared to venture their lives for one side or the other to make civil war a feasible proposition.

There were, in fact, civilian forces in England and Wales, known as the Trained Bands (the term 'militia' only then coming into use). These had undergone considerable reorganisation under the Tudors, and the country divided into zones of military importance, the most important of which came under the control of the Parliament in 1642. Had the readiness and preparedness of the Bands been as it ought to have been, then at the start of the civil war Parliament's recruiting areas should have provided the best troops, the King's the least impressive. Edgehill indicated that this was not the case. Like all civilian armed forces, their quality depended much upon their sense of commitment and that of their officers, and these were variable throughout the country. The Trained Bands could encompass anyone between 16 and 60 years of age of sufficient social standing to be entrusted with arms for the defence of the Kingdom. Although monthly training schedules were expected, in reality some Bands hardly met together at all, and then often only for convivial reasons. Under Tudor military reforms, responsibility for the Trained Bands had been vested in the Lords Lieutenant of counties, usually the most powerful nobleman resident in a county or else appointed because of his general standing. In the 1580s the Lieutenant had been made responsible for the appointment and pay of professional soldiers, known as Muster Masters, whose task was to train and discipline the local levies. Given a lethargic attitude on the part of the Lord Lieutenant or his deputies, and an overall lack of urgency in the international situation, a general neglect followed. Local gentry often sought to avoid the financial implications of office in their Band, but their involvement was essential. The whole concept of the Band was that it should reflect the social order in arms; officered by the gentry, with yeomen, small farmers and others of reasonable standing acting as non-commissioned officers and the rank and file. Largely due to the local nature of these forces, therefore, even when they were in any state of readiness, they were reluctant and often would not march far from their home base. Even the best Trained Bands, those of London, which turned back the royalist army at Turnham Green in November 1642, proved wilful and sometimes mutinous when marched away to the West as part of a larger army. They were, on the whole, the London Bands included, notoriously unreliable, yet these were the forces to whom Parliament and the King were obliged to turn in 1642 to provide at least the core of an army.

Parliament had taken upon itself the right to raise and dispose of armed forces within the Kingdom, through the powers of the Militia Ordinance of 1642, which the King rightly saw as an act of supreme defiance of his own authority in the military sphere. Attempts to raise the Trained Bands in 1642 by the Parliament and by the King often led to unhappy divisions within county Bands themselves. For example, when the parliamentarian governor of Hull raised Trained Bands from its locality to add muscle to his refusal to admit the King to the port, Charles retaliated by raising other Yorkshire Trained Bands to use against those in Hull. It was widely reported in the summer of 1642 that when the King's Bands were sent into service against the port, they went reluctantly: presumably because the Trained Bands were not expected nor intended to fight against each other, and because the confusion over just who exercised legitimate military authority in England rendered all their actions open to questions of legality. Clearly, Trained Bands of any one county could not be expected to fight against each other in a civil war, even supposing those available were capable of achieving anything.

Parliament's Militia Ordinance, whether or not it was itself a legal instrument for raising men, followed the prescribed form. Instructions were issued to the Lords Lieutenant to raise the Bands, who in their turn delegated the task to their deputies, gentry of substance within a given county who might also be Trained Band commanders themselves. The King countered this with the Commission of Array, an ancient means of levying troops which bypassed the Lord Lieutenant (if he were unreliable) and gave direct instruction to the county sheriff to mobilise forces. The Commission of Array not only empowered the raising of the Bands, but also the raising of volunteer regiments, and it was on the formation of volunteer armies that the civil war was prosecuted by both sides. The Trained Bands, unless their colonels actively brought them in on one side or the other, often found themselves stripped of their arms and equipment in favour of the volunteer units, and whilst the Bands themselves more or less melted away, numbers of their members enlisted in volunteer regiments. Certain Bands did survive well into the civil war: one regiment of Yorkshire Trained Bands, brought over to the King by its colonel, Lord Conyers and Darcy, fought valiantly in 1643 on its way south to Oxford, and in 1645 Cornish Trained Bands were still serving in Hopton's western royalist army. The importance to the Parliament of the London Bands has already been indicated.

The creation of volunteer forces did not entirely break with the Trained Band concept. Like the Bands, these had regional, county or district origins, but unlike the Bands, the volunteer infantrymen or cavalrymen were paid to fight wheresoever they were commanded to go, and on the whole could be relied upon to follow their orders. Thus volunteer regiments raised largely if not entirely in Yorkshire and Durham by the King's general there, the earl of Newcastle, ultimately saw service down south with the Oxford army, and visited all theatres of the war over the next few years. The volunteer armies made the civil war possible, indeed they may be said to have prolonged it, and since at the start of the wars anyway, there was a considerable degree of balance numerically between both armies, it must be clear that, whether men knew what they were fighting for or not, there was no shortage of men prepared to fight. Like the Bands, also, the volunteer regiments were known by the names of their commanders, their colonels: the more popular or prestigious an officer, the more likely he would be to at least maintain his regimental strength in relation to other regiments, even though he might not reach the prescribed strength for his regiment, whether of infantry, cavalry or dragoons. As the war dragged on, so both sides resorted to impressment to boost their numbers, even drafting in captured prisoners of war, but this was largely an unsuccessful procedure, and probably led to more desertions than had been the case when the armies were genuinely and largely volunteer in structure. It is certainly the case that mutiny or near-mutiny was not an uncommon feature in both armies, attributable not only to reluctance to fight, but to want of pay or poor conditions as well. Nor was mutiny necessarily confined to the meaner sorts of men who made up the infantry regiments. Even so prestigious a force as the Northern Horse, officered entirely by gentry and with many troopers of good social standing, came near to mutiny in 1645 because it wanted to go back and fight in Yorkshire rather than stay with the King's main Oxford army. In this case, the potential mutineers were given leave to go to Yorkshire, where they performed prodigiously, but most potential mutinies were averted one way or another. To balance the picture, there was also evidence of a very marked self-sacrificing approach to the war on both sides by various regiments. Newcastle's Whitecoats, for example, died almost to a man on Marston Moor in 1644 rather than surrender to Cromwell, and many last stands were recorded up and down the country by small bodies of men, particularly garrisons of castles and houses taken by storm who had had the opportunity to surrender and escape slaughter. Rupert's cavalry, which could charge so well and to such effect on most occasions, turned tail and fled from Marston Moor despite all his efforts to rally them. They were essentially an elite. Cornish regiments stormed Lansdown Hill in 1643 and plucked victory out of a potential rout by virtue of their dogged determination and the example of their commander, who died at their head. When all around them had fled in panic, a Scottish regiment of horse stood its ground on Marston Moor until it was overwhelmed.

The successful record of particular regiments depended very much upon their *esprit de corps*, upon the leadership they received from their colonel and the two other field commanders, the lieutenant colonel and the major. The success of armies depended upon the quality of generals, and by and large the armies of the civil war years were commanded by a strange assortment of men. The King's best generals were probably Ralph Hopton, before the war an opponent of royal policy, and Jacob Astley. Parliament had the earl of Essex, much-underrated by historians, but despite Lostwithiel a competent man beloved by his army, and, of course, Cromwell, who rose to prominence from mid-1644 onwards. Sir Thomas Fairfax, like Prince Rupert, had his days, although he was probably a better army commander than was Rupert, whose capacity for alienating those of his own side was almost as great as his capacity for inspiring loyalty amongst his chosen subordinates. The royalist earl of Newcastle was reckoned to be too much of a poet to command an army, but he chose his advisers reasonably astutely, and there is no doubt that the parliamentarian earl of Manchester, so detested by Cromwell, was a soldier's general as much as was Essex. Individual regimental commanders stood out on both sides. The royalist Sir William Vaughan, the 'Devil of Shrawardine', the royalist Sir Marmaduke Langdale, commander of the Northern Horse, and the parliamentarians Sir John Meldrum and John Lambert. What is often not recognised is the fact that on the whole, there was quite a considerable array of military talent available in the civil war years, partly if not wholly due to the wide experience gained by many civil war commanders in the wars in Europe. As it happened, the majority of those semi-professional commanders opted to serve the King, although the royalists lost a chance to have the services of Edward Massey, the successful parliamentarian governor of Gloucester. If, man for man as has been suggested, the royalist commanders were the best of the bunch, parliamentarian resilience saved them from defeat, coupled with the inability of the royalists to capitalise upon their early successes and the forging of the military alliance with the Scots in 1643. If the Scots did nothing else to assist Parliament (and that was a matter for argument then as now) they helped break the King's northern royalist army beyond repair, and contributed to tying down other royalist forces whilst the Parliament, given a breathing space, got on with winning its war.

Prescribed regimental strengths were hardly ever attained or, if reached, rarely maintained. The number for an infantry regiment was reckoned to be around 1,300 men divided into ten *companies*,

100 in each for the captains' companies, 140 in the majors', 160 in the lieutenant colonels' and 200 in the colonels'. Inferior company officers were lieutenant, ensign, two sergeants, three corporals and two drummers. Each company was two-thirds musketeers and one-third pikemen. Horse regiments were reckoned to be around 500 strong. They were the same in both armies, with six *troops* commanded by field officers (i.e. major, lieutenant colonel or colonel), with lieutenants, cornets, quartermasters, corporals and trumpeters under them. Parliamentary regiments, however, had no lieutenant colonels. This was true for dragoons also, although dragoons (mounted infantry) as often as not formed troops within cavalry regiments or worked as units of less than regimental strength. The royalist army was particularly weak in dragoons in 1642/3, and very few purely dragoon regiments have been identified. It was the responsibility of the commissioned colonel of a regiment, and of his subordinate field officers, to recruit the regiment to somewhere near a respectable size often, since the war treasuries were rarely adequately supplied with money, financing forces from his own pocket. One of the factors which cut the numbers of men in the royalist army in 1644/5 was the inability of the individual colonel to continue to find money from his own pocket, particularly if he were a gentleman reliant upon his rent rolls whose estate had been overrun by parliamentarians and the money due from it converted to the service of the Parliament in one way or another. Certain royalist regiments more or less melted away as a consequence of this, and the financial problem certainly militated against the King more than it did against Parliament. Naturally, one of the inducements to bring volunteers into a regiment was the rate of pay offered, but pay was sometimes as much as two years in arrears, and plunder and free quarter were the only means which the bulk of the rank and file had of keeping body and soul together. War weariness was as much attributable to lack of pay as anything else, and soldiers tended to wander off despite the punishment for desertion, if they could find no other inducement to stay.

It may well appear that the war effort of both sides was a pretty ramshackle affair. Although some efforts were made, and sometimes successfully, to equip troops with 'uniforms' of distinctive colour, battlefield plunder and downright theft probably gave a regiment at the end of a campaign a somewhat motley appearance. Whilst there was a good deal of courage displayed on both sides, desertion in battle and at other times was a constant problem for commanders, as was mutiny. Cromwell himself was in fear of his life at least once from mutinous troops, and part of the disarray of the parliamentarian army at Edgehill may be attributed to the desertion *en masse* of the regiment commanded by Faithful Fortescue, who went over to the King's side as battle was joined. As shortage of money made itself felt, and with lack of adequate provisions, soldiers began to live off the countryside, their treatment of the civilian population reflecting their own desperation. In the war-torn regions of the South-West and the Welsh border, it was hardly surprising that country people should band together against the depredations of both armies, sometimes with success. For the most part country people themselves, the rank and file, would often drift off homewards at harvest time, although how far this was a serious problem is difficult to quantify. Evidence suggests that those most likely to volunteer for military service would be the surplus mouths of a community, under-worked younger sons and brothers, or wilder spirits tired of their rural life style. They might be likely to plunder a harvest field but hardly likely to go home to help get one in, unless it made a good excuse to take a few weeks leave. Once these troops were committed to battle, however elaborately or well laid the plans of their generals might be, all turned upon circumstance whether a regiment stood and fought or turned and ran, and the qualities of the regimental and company or troop commanders were of the highest importance. The generals might well propose, but it was the inferior officers who could dispose by their attention to their duty. One side of a battlefield might as well have been a hundred miles from the other side, so entirely isolated in their efforts were the men involved. At Marston Moor the Scottish and parliamentarian commanders in chief fled the field because they saw their own right wing scattered by a royalist charge, and it was Cromwell, cavalry well in hand, who swept around the field and undid the damage done by that royalist assault. The Scottish general was twenty miles away or more when he heard the news, but it is not apparent that either he or his fellow generals were reproached. Within the limitations of the battlefield, they did what they saw as necessary or opportune: all turned ultimately on what their subordinates in the thick of the fight did, and how successful they were. Lacking all the technical equipment which modern armies possess to inform themselves of the progress of events (although no guarantee against errors of judgement in themselves) civil war commanders threw their forces into the hands of fate every time they resolved upon battle, and no single civil war engagement can be singled out as a foregone conclusion, unless it be a minor ambush or a well co-ordinated surprise raid on sleeping enemy troops.

The Structure of the Atlas

In the following maps and accompanying commentaries, the reader is taken through the civil wars chronologically. A few maps show the state of the country overall at certain periods. Most maps look at particular regions where fighting was widespread, outlining the key stages of the fighting in those regions. These maps show the development of campaigns, the sites of battles, sieges and skirmishes. Some maps consider particularly important battles. For each battle there are generally two maps, one showing the locality and the precise site of the battle in relation to surrounding villages, the second showing the field itself in more detail and illustrating the action and the movements of the armies. Maps covering events in Scotland and Ireland are included also.

For each map there is a page of commentary which provides relevant background and an outline of the events portrayed on the map. The standard symbol for a battle site has been used and dates on the maps indicate the date of a battle, the fall of a town, the entry of an army into a particular town, as appropriate. Counties referred to are, of course, the pre-1974 counties.

ATLAS OF THE ENGLISH CIVIL WAR

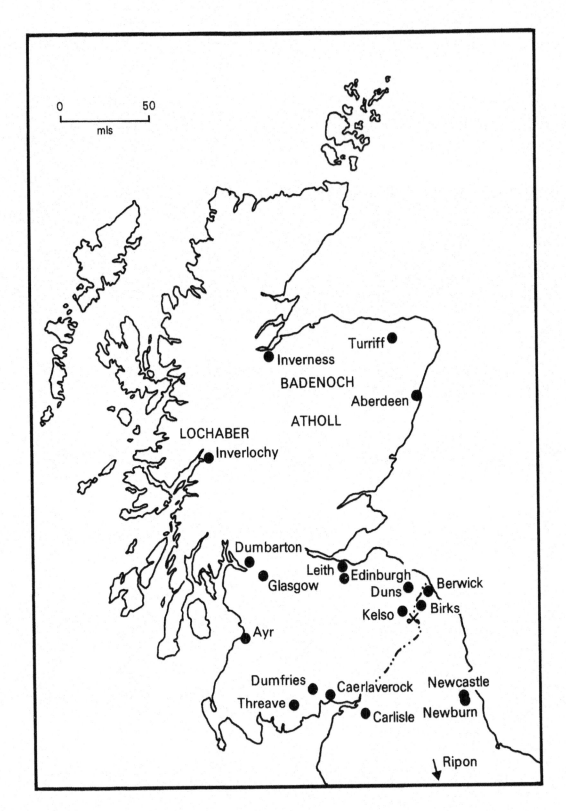

0　　50
mls

Turriff

Inverness

BADENOCH

Aberdeen

ATHOLL

LOCHABER

Inverlochy

Dumbarton

Leith

Edinburgh

Berwick

Glasgow

Duns

Birks

Kelso

Ayr

Dumfries

Caerlaverock

Newcastle

Threave

Carlisle

Newburn

Ripon

MAP 1 Scotland in 1639–1640 and the Bishops' Wars

The root cause of the armed confrontations between Charles I and part of his Scottish subjects lay in his policy of anglicisation and their fears that the union of the two crowns was leading them into subjugation. As early as 1637 there were hopes of a closer, parliamentary union, to offset the personal union represented by Charles, but internal divisions and contradictions led Scotland first to ally with Parliament in 1643, then to revert to loyalty to the Crown and, as a consequence, to end up as a military occupied country from 1651 until 1660. Nevertheless, Scottish resistance to the King encouraged that of Englishmen in 1642, as did the inability of the King effectively to counter Scottish insurgence. By February 1639 'hostilities' had begun in Scotland: at Inverness royalist arms supplies raised for the marquis of Huntly were seized, and shortly afterwards covenanting troops drove royalist forces off from Turriff. Aberdeen was surrendered to Montrose, a covenanting general, and only Threave and Caerlaverock Castles on the border remained in loyal hands. Charles intended to raise 30,000 men to take into Scotland, but recruiting was slow, and he was advised to wait a year. Despite the advice, Charles was determined to invade Scotland, and to send the marquis of Hamilton by sea to the Firth of Forth. Charles was at York on 30 March, whilst Hamilton lay at Yarmouth with 5,000 men ready to sail. He anchored before Leith on 1 May but the covenanters were obdurate, and the King hesitated in his plans. On 14 May he reached Newcastle, whilst Scottish royalists occupied Turriff and Aberdeen (the latter briefly). On the 30th Charles lay at Birks near Berwick with 20,000 men, with forward troops across the border at Duns. This manoeuvre caused the Covenanters to advance on Kelso, which they held on 3 June against a counter-attack. Two days later the Scottish army came to Duns and offered to negotiate with Charles, who agreed, but away north Aberdeen was again occupied by royalist troops and had to be stormed by Montrose on 18 and 19 June. On the 18th, the two sides reached agreement at Berwick, termed a treaty but to all intents and purposes merely a truce. When the Short Parliament met on 13 April 1640 plans for the reduction of Scotland were laid before it. The Commons proved unwilling to be coerced into sanctioning further military efforts, and Parliament was dissolved on 5 May. Urged on by Strafford, Charles was bent upon the suppression of Scotland, raising a new army under the earl of Northumberland. Within Scotland, only Threave, Caerlaverock, Edinburgh and Dumbarton were in royalist hands, and on the day that the Short Parliament was dissolved covenanting troops entered Aberdeen, centre of royalist resistance. With the Scottish Parliament sitting against royal wishes, and forces being raised, Covenanters overran Atholl, Badenoch and Lochaber in June, causing Montrose, suspicious of the Covenanters' objectives, to side with the threatened royalist Lord Ogilvie.

Meanwhile the main Scottish army began to assemble on the border with England, and the invasion of England was decided upon on 3 August. This finally drove Montrose and other former Covenanters into open rift with their party, but too late to alter the course of events. On 20 August, as the King left London for the north, the Scottish army rolled across the border into Northumberland and came to Newburn on the Tyne on 27 August. Resistance from the English troops was patchy and ineffectual, and on 30 August Newcastle upon Tyne was occupied without difficulty by the Scottish army. In their rear, Dumbarton had fallen, Caerlaverock was undergoing vigorous siege, and in September Lord Ettrick was to surrender Edinburgh into covenanting hands. Helpless, Charles summoned a Great Council to York for 24 September, Parliament was summoned to meet on 3 November, and on 2 October negotiations began at Ripon with the Scots which were to lead to the Treaty of Ripon. By this, the Scots occupied Northumberland and Durham with a daily subsidy of £850 to support them until problems were finally hammered out with the sitting of Parliament in London.

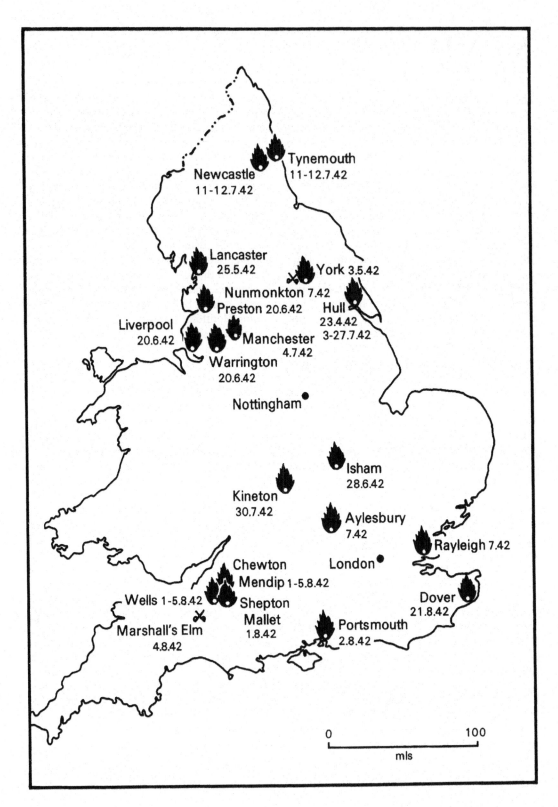

Newcastle
11-12.7.42

Tynemouth
11-12.7.42

Lancaster
25.5.42

York 3.5.42

Nunmonkton 7.42

Preston 20.6.42

Hull
23.4.42
3-27.7.42

Liverpool
20.6.42

Manchester
4.7.42

Warrington
20.6.42

Nottingham

Isham
28.6.42

Kineton
30.7.42

Aylesbury
7.42

Rayleigh 7.42

London

Chewton
Mendip 1-5.8.42

Wells 1-5.8.42

Shepton
Mallet
1.8.42

Dover
21.8.42

Marshall's Elm
4.8.42

Portsmouth
2.8.42

0   100

mls

MAP 2 Flashpoints of Civil War in the Summer of 1642

Although civil war did not formally break out until the King raised his standard on 22 August 1642 at Nottingham, the summer had seen both sides flexing their muscles and striving for advantage on a localised level. The physical division between the King and his Parliament came in March, when Charles arrived in the city of York on the 18th of that month and established his court there. It was in Yorkshire that first overt royalist action took place when, on 3 May, Sir Francis Wortley reportedly drew his sword and swore to maintain the King against his Parliament, and began to raise 200 horse for the royal service. The Trained Band regiment of Robert Strickland was then brought into York to serve as a royal Lifeguard. In Lancashire on 25 May a gathering of local Catholic gentry near Lancaster was dispersed by the High Sheriff, a royalist, as being premature, but on 20 June agents of the Lord Strange seized magazines in Preston, Warrington and Liverpool. On 4 July Strange attacked the puritan town of Manchester in some force but was driven off after inconclusive fighting. From York, on 20 June, the earl of Newcastle, future royalist commander in the north, was sent to secure the port of Newcastle upon Tyne and Tynemouth and with them the Northumberland and Durham coalfield. This, despite a minor rising by colliers on 11/12 July, he succeeded in doing. The King, having been refused entry to Hull in April, advanced on the port from York on 3 July, and on the 10th the first fighting took place. Hull was besieged from the 15th, but on the 27th Sir John Meldrum, the garrison commander, raided Strickland's regiment at Anlaby, outside Hull, and inflicted severe casualties. The King abandoned the profitless siege.

Somerset also saw some early action. On 11 July the marquess of Hertford was sent there from York by the King to raise men, and on the 19th Parliament sent Alexander Popham to do the same on its behalf. From 28 July, Wells became the royalist mustering town, whilst from the 30th the Parliament's friends gathered at Shepton Mallet. On 1 August occurred an ugly brawl in the latter town when Sir Ralph Hopton met up with William Strode MP. This developed into an armed confrontation between local country people, raised by the Sheriff as a posse comitatus, and the royalist forces. Nothing came of it, but Hertford's commission as lieutenant general became official on 2 August, and on the 3rd he sent troops into Shepton Mallet and beyond to the foot of the Mendips in a show of strength. After plundering the town of weapons, the royalists withdrew to Wells. Elsewhere in the county, Strode and John Pyne on behalf of the Parliament were seeking to combine their separate forces, to move against Wells. The royalists acted pre-emptively to prevent their conjunction, and at the battle of Marshall's Elm fought on 4 August, the royalists routed and destroyed Pyne's column of 600 men although outnumbered by them. Nevertheless, the Parliament's local forces began to muster at Chewton Mendip to the number of 10,000 to 12,000, far more than Hertford could dispose of to resist them. On the 5th, therefore, the marquess withdrew without offering battle, making his way towards Glastonbury.

As well as these formalised developments, there were reports of riots and affrays in Rayleigh, Essex; Aylesbury, Buckinghamshire; and Isham in Northamptonshire. On 30 July royalist supporters gathered together on Kineton Heath in Warwickshire to prevent the parliamentary gentry from removing artillery from Banbury to Warwick Castle. Confrontation was avoided when the parliamentary commander, Lord Brooke, agreed to leave the guns in Banbury. Elsewhere on 2 August, George Goring the governor of Portsmouth delivered the port up to the King's supporters, but for no apparent reason he was to abandon it in September and become a field commander for the King. Dover Castle was taken by Parliament on 21 August, the day before the royal standard was unfurled.

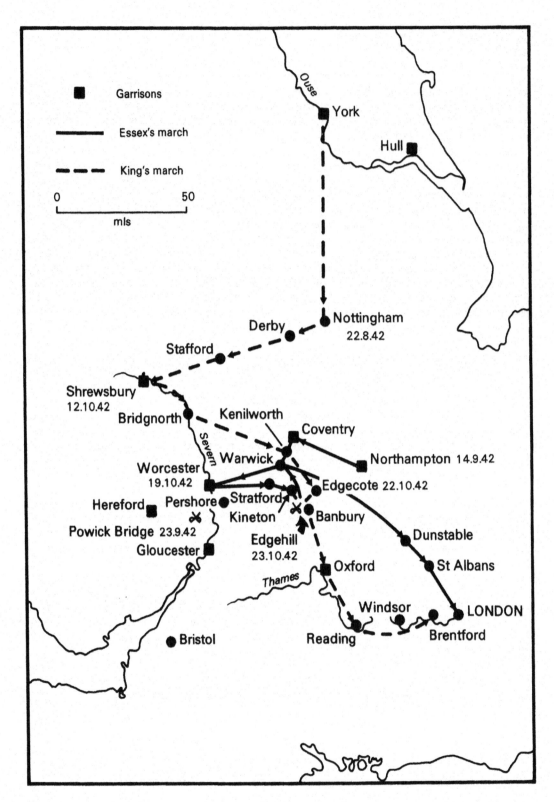

Garrisons

Essex's march

King's march

0   50

mls

Ouse

York

Hull

Nottingham
22.8.42

Derby

Stafford

Shrewsbury
12.10.42

Bridgnorth

Kenilworth

Coventry

Severn

Warwick

Northampton 14.9.42

Worcester
19.10.42

Edgecote 22.10.42

Hereford

Pershore

Stratford

Kineton

Banbury

Powick Bridge 23.9.42

Edgehill
23.10.42

Dunstable

Gloucester

St Albans

Thames

Oxford

Windsor

LONDON

Bristol

Reading

Brentford

MAP 3 1642: Prelude to Edgehill

With the raising of the royal standard on 22 August at Nottingham, amidst inauspicious beginnings, formal war was declared on the Parliament. After recruiting forces at York, the King had moved to Nottingham to increase his power, preparatory to a march on London and an anticipated rapid victory. From Nottingham, however, he marched westwards to Shrewsbury, to the rich recruiting grounds of Wales and the borders. The army of the Parliament under the earl of Essex, appointed Captain General on 13 July, was drawn largely from London and the Home Counties, and when mustered at Northampton (an ideal place for securing footwear for the men) on 14 September (six days before the King entered Shrewsbury) was superior in strength to its opponents. Morale was another question. The first real test for detachments of the two armies was to take place on 23 September.

Although lying between London and the King, the earl of Essex determined to move west also, and to take the city of Worcester. The King initially sought to strengthen the city by sending Prince Rupert with mounted troops to reinforce Sir John Byron there, but the defences were wholly inadequate, and Rupert ordered withdrawal. To forestall a surprise attack during the evacuation, Rupert moved his forces forward to Powick Bridge. Unknown to him, at the same time a parliamentarian force of about the same strength under Colonel John Brown, was detached from Essex's army to rendezvous with Gloucestershire forces reported to be advancing on Worcester. Early on 23 September, Brown's forces appeared south of Powick Bridge but were ignorant of the proximity of the Prince, as he was of their presence. There were counsels of caution for Brown, but he determined to march on, since the main army of the Parliament was itself drawing closer to the city. As the parliamentarian advance guard crossed the bridge, they were met by fierce musket fire, under cover of which the royalist cavalry mounted up ready for action. Edwin Sandys, commanding the parliamentary vanguard, pushed on, and was charged with devastating effect as he sought to deploy beyond the bridge. Scattered at one blow, the fugitives of the vanguard collided with Brown's main body, and in their panic fled until they came up with the earl of Essex's Lifeguard regiment near Pershore. John Brown was able to hinder royalist pursuit, but the damage was done, and the first cavalry victory had gone to Rupert.

Powick Bridge was a much-needed morale booster for the royal army, and saw the birth of the legend of Rupert's invincibility. King Charles, encouraged by the success and the captured colours brought to him, set out from Shrewsbury on 12 October, again aiming for London. Although his army was still smaller than that of Essex, the earl's strength was depleted by his need to garrison strategic towns — Worcester, Hereford, Northampton and Coventry — and the earl showed a fateful indecisiveness. There was also the problem to be overcome of facing the King in arms in the field, and the consequence of failure once that was done. The earl quit Worcester on 19 October to put himself again between the King and London, and both armies now moved slowly, bogged down by treacherous weather conditions. It was also evident that neither side quite knew where the other was, and the factor of poor intelligence dogged both sides throughout the civil war.

On 22 October royalist forces entered Edgecote near Banbury, and a rest was ordered for twenty-four hours, whilst forces were to be detached to assault the enemy garrison at Banbury. Whilst the royalists prepared to establish billets in the general vicinity, a party of Prince Rupert's foragers clashed with parliamentary foragers at Wormleighton. The royalists had the advantage of surprise, and a reconnaissance party set out for Kineton. They discovered the proximity of the bulk of Essex's army, and reported back. Orders were issued for the royalist army to draw into battle order on Edgehill on 23 October.

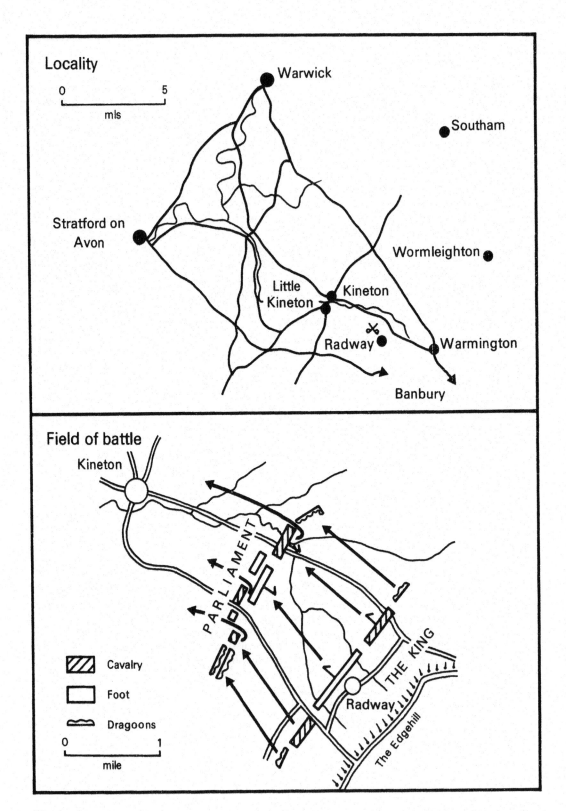

Locality

0 ____ 5
mls

Warwick

Southam

Stratford on Avon

Wormleighton

Little Kineton

Kineton

Radway

Warmington

Banbury

Field of battle

Kineton

PARLIAMENT

THE KING

Radway

The Edgehill

Cavalry

Foot

Dragoons

0 ____ 1
mile

Battle between the two armies was inevitable, but the time and place a matter of chance. From the bare Edgehill a plain ran down towards Kineton township, giving the royalist commanders overall view of the field, but obstructed by enclosures near Kineton itself. Prince Rupert rode to the ridge early in the morning, his cavalry were in place shortly before noon, and the infantry came into position by about two o'clock. Essex's surprise may be indicated by the fact that the royal army was now drawn up between him and London, the position in which the earl had sought to put himself. Nevertheless, the King could not advance with Essex left unharmed in his rear. The earl was advised of the royalist dispositions by eight in the morning, but his own army was strung out in various quarters, and he was in no hurry to fight. Reinforcements were also anticipated. If the worst came to the worst he could fall back on Warwick, whilst Banbury garrison remained unmolested.

The leisurely way in which battle was prepared for allowed time for the rival commanders to concentrate upon tactics, many of the royalists at least having had considerable European war experience. Prince Rupert succeeded in offending the King's Lord General, the earl of Lindsey, in an argument about the merits of employing the Dutch or Swedish tactical plans: Lindsey resigned and went to join his regiment as a mere colonel, when the King supported Rupert. The Prince then moved to join the royalist right wing of cavalry, whilst Henry Wilmot commanded the left. After a desultory cannonade from both sides causing few casualties but much smoke and noise, royalist dragoons moved forward to clear parliamentarian musketeers from hedges on the flanks of the parliamentary army, and then Rupert advanced his wing. The cavalry opposed to him, that of Sir James Ramsey, at first stood stock still, then turned and fled after one of their troops changed sides. Rupert advanced into Kineton where there was considerable killing, whilst his second line under Sir John Byron, galloped off wildly in pursuit of the fugitives. On the left, Wilmot's cavalry scattered the regiment of Lord Feilding, and Wilmot's second in command, Lord Digby, imitated Byron, giving pursuit with gusto. Thus the bulk of the royalist cavalry to all intents and purposes galloped off the field.

The royalist foot advanced under Sir Jacob Astley, and the parliamentary foot under Charles Essex broke before they engaged. Fresh troops under Thomas Ballard filled the gap, and two cavalry units, unaffected by Rupert's or Wilmot's charges, were brought into use against Astley's infantry. There was general disruption as some of the parliamentary horse succeeded in reaching and disabling some of the royalist artillery in the rear, but they soon fell back, only to be fired upon by their own men who mistook them for royalists.

The earl of Essex launched a severe assault on the brigade of Sir Nicholas Byron, and in this fighting the earl of Lindsey was killed, his son standing guard over the body until he fell into parliamentary hands. The royal standard was cut from the hands of its bearer, Sir Edmund Verney, and carried away. A royalist charge under Sir Charles Lucas became caught up in the pursuit of fugitives, and came to nothing. Captain John Smith, separated from Lucas's formation, ran into a party of parliamentarian soldiers carrying the royal standard away, attacked single-handed and recaptured the flag. Meanwhile, meeting resistance from some parliamentarian forces, Prince Rupert's cavalry began to drift back to the battlefield, and their presence caused the infantry to stiffen. Despite advice to the contrary, Rupert chose not to charge again, and night fell on what is generally considered to have been a stalemated battlefield, where total losses were about 3,000 men in all. On the day following, the earl of Essex retreated to Warwick, leaving the road to London wide open to the King's army. In essence, if he could now capitalise upon it, Charles I had won a strategic advantage.

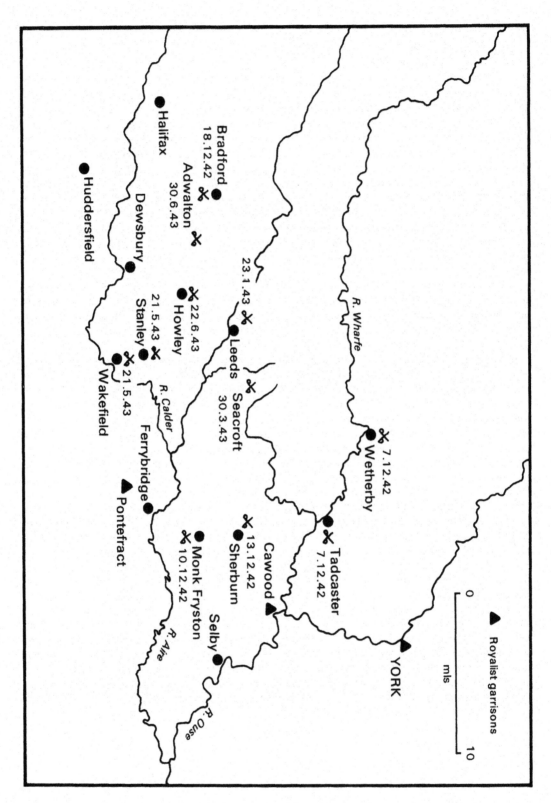

Halifax

Bradford
18.12.42

Adwalton
30.6.43

Huddersfield

Dewsbury

23.1.43

21.5.43
Stanley

22.6.43
Howley

Leeds

Seacroft
30.3.43

Wakefield
21.5.43

Ferrybridge

Pontefract

R. Calder

R. Wharfe

7.12.42
Wetherby

13.12.42
Sherburn

Cawood

Tadcaster
7.12.42

Monk Fryston
10.12.42

Selby

R. Aire

R. Ouse

YORK

▲ Royalist garrisons

0   mls   10

MAP 6 1642-1643: War in Yorkshire and the North-East

From the summer of 1642, Northumberland and Durham were firmly under royalist control, and until 1644 Yorkshire was the scene of actual fighting. When the King left York, the royalist commander, the earl of Cumberland, proved himself loyal but incapable of resisting the Fairfaxes and their allies. Until December 1642, the royalists were on the defensive, but as a result of an agreement between Yorkshire royalists and the earl of Newcastle, the latter marched into the county in that month to take overall control. He brought a well disciplined and well trained army, and the parliamentary forces hovered around their strongholds — Scarborough, Hull and the West Riding cloth towns — instead of raiding at will. The earl's objective was ostensibly to destroy resistance in the county, and then march south towards London in support of the King's army. To this end he set up major garrisons to divide Hull from the cloth towns, and pushed down into Lincolnshire and Nottinghamshire. On 23 January 1643, however, Sir Thomas Fairfax struck back, taking Leeds. The earl was deflected for a while by the arrival at Bridlington of the Queen with arms and munitions for the main army, but her arrival led to the defection of Sir Hugh Cholmeley from the Parliament, and Scarborough passed into royalist hands. In Hull, the Hothams were thought to be considering a similar move. Lord Fairfax consolidated around Leeds, and Sir Thomas went forward to destroy Tadcaster bridge. Unable to prevent royalist cavalry under George Goring from crossing the Wharfe, Sir Thomas began to fall back but was caught at Seacroft Moor on 30 March and his infantry suffered heavy losses. The royalists took numerous prisoners, and Sir Thomas Fairfax left them to their fate.

In May he struck back, launching a surprise assault on the garrison town of Wakefield held by numerically superior forces under Goring. After savage fighting in the streets, Goring was taken with the bulk of his infantry, and the royalists fled the town. The earl of Newcastle, concerned for the safety of the Queen on her way to Oxford, finally had his hands free in early June. On the 22nd of that month he stormed Howley House, a major parliamentarian strongpoint in the West Riding, and on 30 June clashed with the main parliamen-tary field army at Adwalton Moor near Bradford. The royalist army, about 10,000 strong, faced 4,000 parliamentarian regulars and a sizeable number of poorly armed countrymen, but initially the parliamentarians had the best of it. A desperate assault by royalist pikemen, however, broke open the parliamentarian lines and a renewed royalist cavalry charge destroyed the cohesion of the parliamentarian left wing. The earl swept on and took Bradford, and Leeds fell when royalist prisoners there broke free and seized arms in the town. The Fairfaxes fled into Hull, where the wavering Hothams had been arrested on suspicion, and the port was thus safeguarded for the Parliament.

No determined march south, however, followed Newcastle's sweeping series of triumphs. After advancing into Lincolnshire to repair damage sustained by royalist forces there, he drew back into Yorkshire, having been advised to deal with Hull before he left the county behind for good. Lord Fairfax had raised substantial troops in the port, and was in contact with forces across the Humber. The second siege of Hull began on 2 September 1643 after the town of Beverley was surprised and Sir Thomas Fairfax chased from it. Lord Fairfax ordered the dykes around Hull to be cut and the lowlying land flooded, occasioning problems for besieged and besieger alike, but a necessary move. The Humber still provided a lifeline for the garrison, and troops moved back and forth across it regularly. Newcastle, now elevated as marquess, ignored advice to move south, and doggedly pursued the siege. There was considerable skirmishing, the royalists fairly safe within their earthworks constructed around the town, but on 11 October the crucial action was fought. Whilst Sir Thomas Fairfax and the Parliament's Eastern Association army won a sweeping victory at Winceby in Lincolnshire, in the aftermath of which the guns of Hull could be heard firing upon the royalists, Lord Fairfax launched a counter-attack. The royalist cavalry were held at bay by the port's cannon, whilst the infantry fought it out in the mud of the earthworks. After severe fighting, the royalists withdrew, and the marquess abandoned the siege, as he had abandoned the idea of a march south.

25

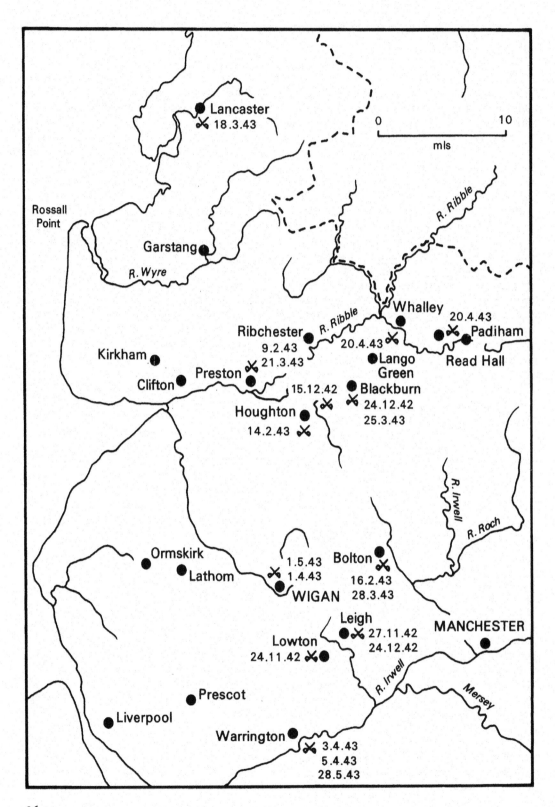

Rossall
Point

Lancaster
18.3.43

0   10
mls

Garstang

R. Wyre

R. Ribble

Whalley   20.4.43
Padiham

Ribchester   *R. Ribble*   20.4.43
9.2.43
21.3.43   Read Hall

Kirkham   Lango
Green

Clifton   Preston   15.12.42   Blackburn
24.12.42
Houghton   25.3.43
14.2.43

R. Irwell

R. Roch

Ormskirk   1.5.43   Bolton
Lathom   1.4.43   16.2.43
WIGAN   28.3.43

Leigh
Lowton   27.11.42   MANCHESTER
24.11.42   24.12.42

Prescot

R. Irwell

Liverpool   *Mersey*

Warrington   3.4.43
5.4.43
28.5.43

MAP 7 1642–1643: War in Lancashire and the North-West

The situation in the North-West almost paralleled that in the North-East. Whilst Cumberland and Westmorland remained more or less under royalist control, the battleground was Lancashire. Numerous incidents in the county during the summer had paved the way for something more dangerous after August 1642, but the royalist commander, the earl of Derby, was deprived of most of his best regiments for service with the King elsewhere. Consequently, he was unable to offer resistance to the parliamentary forces based on Manchester. A siege of that town, begun on 24 September, was abandoned by the earl on 2 October, and tentative truce talks were initiated. These failed, and a series of localised skirmishes ensued. The royalists consolidated around Preston, Wigan and Warrington, setting up headquarters in the latter town. Whilst busy recruiting in November, the earl raided into Cheshire without success, and a form of stalemate prevailed in Lancashire until early into 1643. An indecisive encounter at Leigh early in December followed a royalist defeat on nearby Hinfield Moor on or around 27 November. The royalist commanders were more concerned about their financial position, and the need to repair losses in men before launching a general war. On 15 December they won a small action on Houghton Common, but on 24 December a royalist garrison put hastily into Leigh was driven out by troops from Manchester. On the same day an attempt by Sir Gilbert Houghton to assault the parliamentarian town of Blackburn was defeated.

On 9 February parliamentarian troops attacked Preston, defended with mud and brick walls, and took the town in a particularly bloody encounter. The war had suddenly taken on new vigour. From Preston on 14 February, the parliamentary forces marched out and took Houghton Tower without a shot, only to suffer losses when a booby-trapped supply of power was set off. On 16 February, the earl of Derby struck back with an attack on Bolton in a 'suddaine and violent manner'. Fierce street fighting followed, but the parliamentarians held firm. Three days later, on 19 February, royalist forces left in Lancaster found themselves under attack from parliamentarian troops from Preston

bent upon fortifying and garrisoning Lancaster and its castle. The royalists withdrew, and carried word to Derby, who determined to bend his power against Lancaster. Decisive action was needed, since the war was closing in on Derby's two main garrisons, Wigan and Warrington. Temporarily reinforced by some old regiments under Viscount Molyneux, and with irregulars from around Kirkham, the earl marched towards Lancaster on 13 March, and summoned the town on the 18th. Fierce fighting led to the town's fall and the garrison retreated into the castle. On 20 March, however, a relief force under Sir John Seaton from Preston took the field, but it was plagued by mutiny, and Derby succeeded in out-manoeuvring it, abandoning Lancaster and instead capturing Preston in Seaton's absence with little resistance. Blackburn also fell to the earl. Parliamentarian field forces were demoralised, and the earl planned to march against Manchester, but was thwarted by the removal of his best regiments to join the Oxford army. Choosing instead to attack Bolton, the royalists assaulted the town on 28 March. They were beaten off. On 1 April parliamentarian troops from Manchester stormed and took Wigan. Bolton was reinforced. Derby, meanwhile, fought and won an encounter at Stockton Heath near Warrington on 3 April, but was deflected from marching on Manchester and was virtually hemmed in around Warrington by a combination of local parliamentary levies and Cheshire men under Brereton. Two days later, the attempt to storm Warrington failed, and both sides marked time again. A single decisive battle was needed, and it was fought on 20 April at Whalley. The day before, royalist troops left Preston for Ribchester and were sighted near Padiham: they were followed until the alarm was raised, whereupon the parliamentarians drew up in force on Read-Bank. An attempt to dislodge them failed, and the retreating royalists fell back on Whalley where the earl was. On Lango Green the royalists were scattered and fell back on Ribchester. All cohesion was lost, and piece by piece Lancashire fell into parliamentarian hands, until only the earl's house at Lathom remained unreduced.

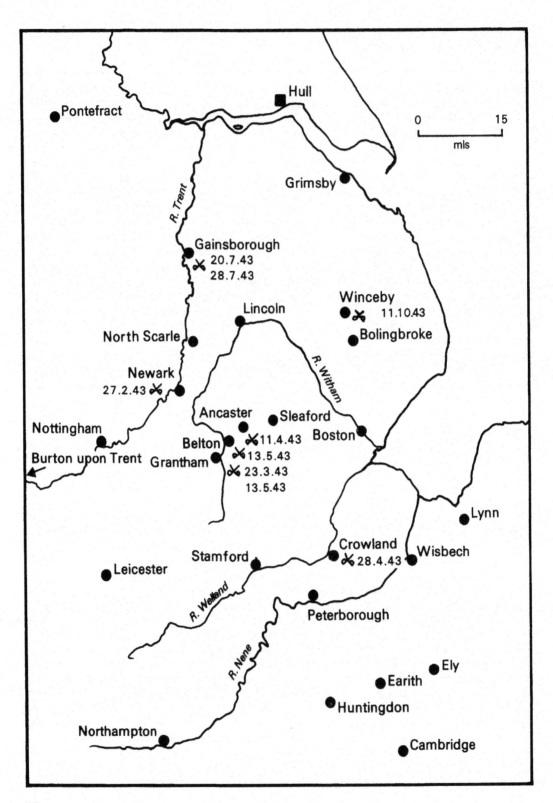

Pontefract

Hull

Grimsby

R. Trent

Gainsborough
20.7.43
28.7.43

Winceby
11.10.43
Bolingbroke

Lincoln

North Scarle

R. Witham

Newark
27.2.43

Ancaster   Sleaford
Belton   11.4.43   Boston
Nottingham   13.5.43
Burton upon Trent   Grantham   23.3.43
13.5.43

Lynn

Crowland
28.4.43   Wisbech

Leicester   Stamford

R. Welland

Peterborough

R. Nene

Ely

Earith

Huntingdon

Northampton

Cambridge

0   15
mls

MAP 8 1642–1643: War in the East and East Midlands

The counties of Norfolk, Suffolk, Essex, Hertfordshire and Cambridgeshire, formed into the Eastern Association on 20 December 1642, saw little real fighting, coming early and easily under parliamentarian control. Lincolnshire and Nottinghamshire were the battlegrounds, where the southward thrusts of the earl of Newcastle were resisted, although Lincolnshire was a markedly royalist county. In early December 1642, Newcastle had garrisoned Pontefract in Yorkshire, and sent forces out to garrison Newark on Trent, a crucially strategic point for north-south communications. In January, the earl depleted the Newark garrison, now reliant on local forces under Sir John Henderson. An attack on the town by Thomas Ballard on 27 February with substantial forces was decisively beaten off, and Newark remained henceforth almost unassailable. From Newark on 23 March royalists under Henderson and Sir Charles Cavendish took Grantham, and on 11 April won the battle of Ancaster Heath against Lord Willoughby of Parham. Alarmed by these successes, the Eastern Association had to react, in fear of Newcastle making a march south with a huge army, reported to be at least 15,000 strong. Oliver Cromwell occupied Peterborough on 22 April and on the 28th stormed Crowland, a minor royalist garrison. On 9 May, in response to alarmed orders from London, Cromwell and forces from Nottinghamshire and Lincolnshire, rendezvoused at Sleaford preparatory to an attack on Newark. They proved somewhat dilatory, however, enabling Cavendish and Henderson to meet secretly with their forces near Grantham for an intended pre-emptive action.

On 13 May the royalists destroyed three parliamentarian cavalry troops at Belton, and then turned to face the main army close to Grantham itself. After a brief exchange of fire, Cromwell charged the royalist horse and seems to have driven them from the field, but his own casualties may well have been heavy, leading to abandonment of the Newark march. The risk of a southward march by Newcastle remained unabated, however, and by late May 1643 the parliamentary troops began to gather in strength around Nottingham. They did nothing, however, to prevent the march of the Queen and her escort towards Oxford, which had entered Newark unopposed and left again on 21 June. On 2 July the royalists took Burton on Trent. The Queen's departure had relieved the earl of Newcastle of a major handicap, and he at once took the field to clear Yorkshire of the Fairfaxes. Sir Charles Cavendish, detached from the Queen, was also active again in Lincolnshire, and laid siege to Gainsborough, taken on 20 July by parliamentary forces under Willoughby. Cromwell and his probable mentor, Sir John Meldrum, were ordered to relieve Gainsborough, and drew up their forces at North Scarle, on 27 July. On the 28th, advance guards of both armies clashed north of the River Lea, and the royalists fell back on their main body. In the bitterly fought action which followed, Cavendish was killed and the royalists broken. Gainsborough was relieved, but the advance of a substantial royalist army (rumoured to be but small) belatedly coming to Cavendish's aid, obliged the parliamentarians to retreat into Lincoln. The earl of Newcastle bombarded and took Gainsborough, and caused the reduction of Lincoln. Cromwell, meanwhile, had fallen back to the Isle of Ely. In August, however, Newcastle marched back into Yorkshire to besiege Hull, and his enemies could move freely again. The new commander in chief of the Eastern Association army, the earl of Manchester, took Lynn on 16 September, and on 5 October sent 500 men to Hull to strengthen it. Joining with Cromwell and Thomas Fairfax at Boston, the earl of Manchester waited upon events. Cavendish's successor as royalist commander, Sir William Widdrington, was advancing with forces from Newark and elsewhere towards Bolingbroke where Manchester had laid siege, and the royalist advance was covered all the way. On 11 October the two armies met at Winceby, resulting in a decisive and costly defeat for the royalists. Newcastle abandoned the siege of Hull partly in consequence of this setback. Gainsborough was evacuated, and Lincoln was taken by parliamentary troops, in the wake of Winceby. Newark remained solidly royalist, however, and an important focal point for subsequent resurrection of royalist activities in the area.

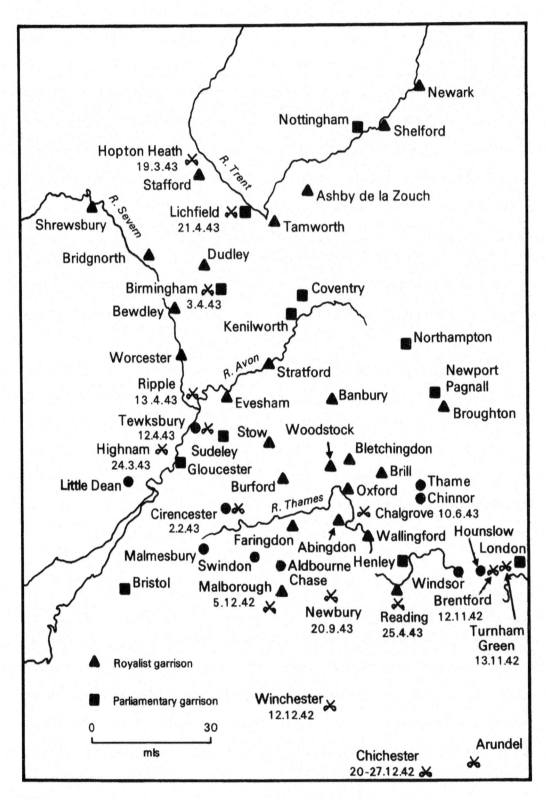

Royalist garrison

Parliamentary garrison

0   30

mls

MAP 9 1642–1643: War in the Centre

Following upon the battle of Edgehill, the King's army took Banbury on 27 October, and then made for Oxford, which became the royal headquarters. From Oxford, the army moved to Reading on 4 November, whilst Essex's army entered London four days later to bolster resistance. On 12 November Prince Rupert attacked Brentford, took the town and inflicted heavy losses on its garrison. London armed rapidly, and the next day 24,000 men under Philip Skippon were drawn up at Turnham Green. The King declined to fight and withdrew to Hounslow, thence to Oxford, occupying neighbouring counties. The university town was extensively fortified, and garrisons set up at Reading, Wallingford, Abingdon, Banbury, Brill, Faringdon and Burford. Both armies appear to have anticipated a quiet winter, but on 5 December Wilmot took Marlborough from the parliamentarians, and the latter under Waller stormed Winchester on the 12th. Essex controlled the Thames valley. Early in 1643 both sides won victories: Rupert took Cirencester on 2 February, Waller seized Arundel and Chichester, becoming commander of the Western Association formed on 11 February. The royalists appeared on the defensive, threatened by Essex from Windsor, with Waller to the west who had taken Malmesbury and broken the marquess of Worcester's small personal army at Highnam on 24 March. The first major action, however, was fought at Hopton Heath on 19 March, where the earl of Northampton, *en route* to relieve Lichfield, confronted parliamentarian forces under Sir John Gell and Sir William Brereton. The parliamentary troops advanced on Stafford, where the earl hastily prepared to receive them. The battle, although it cost the earl of Northampton his life, was a royalist victory, largely due to ineptitude on the part of Gell and Brereton. Prince Rupert hastily sought to repair the damage of the earl's death, taking Birmingham on 3 April and capturing Lichfield on 21 April, removing a threat to Oxford's communications. Rupert's brother Maurice, however, sought to break Waller's army, which was enjoying successes in South Wales: he failed to do so at Little Dean, and Waller joined Edward Massey, governor of Gloucester, in time to take Tewkesbury on 12 April. Prince Maurice pursued, crossed the Severn,

and took up position at Ripple on 13 April, blocking Waller s advance to Worcester. Although cautious, Maurice was an able tactician, and when Waller began to withdraw, delivered a mighty blow as the parliamentarian force moved along a narrow lane. Waller's men fled almost to Tewkesbury, where fresh troops halted royalist pursuit. Maurice then marched to Oxford, to assist in saving Reading from the earl of Essex, who nevertheless took the crucial town on 25 April. Thereafter, Maurice and the marquess of Hertford were despatched to the West Country, and Waller with his army also shifted that way, relieving pressure on Oxford.

From Reading on 10 June Essex marched to Thame. Rupert with a small force sought to capture Essex's army pay-train near Chinnor, but failed. Withdrawing, he was threatened by parliamentarian pursuit, and drew up in Chalgrove Field near Chislehampton Bridge, which he secured. The battle was a royalist victory, and led to the death of the MP, John Hampden, and to growing dissatisfaction with the earl of Essex at London. The King now moved against Gloucester, summoning it on 10 August and then laying siege. The earl of Essex left London to relieve the city, and brushed aside an attempt to stop him at Stow on the Wold early in September. The King abandoned the siege, and Essex now had somehow to return with army intact, to London. He reached Cirencester on 15 September and Swindon on the 17th, the royalists marching parallel with him. On the 18th the earl was held up at Aldbourne Chase by Rupert and, moving very slowly, entered Newbury where royalist cavalry at once made a brief stunning raid. The battle of Newbury, fought on 20 September took place south of the town, with King Charles in personal command of the royalist army, and Newbury itself in his hands. The battle was a stalemate, but the King withdrew towards Oxford and the earl of Essex, harried by cavalry, reached London safely. Nevertheless, Essex's survival was the only bright spot for Parliament in 1643, for elsewhere the royalists had scored major strategic successes, and on paper at least appeared poised to win the war by a concerted assault on the Home Counties and London from north, north-west and west.

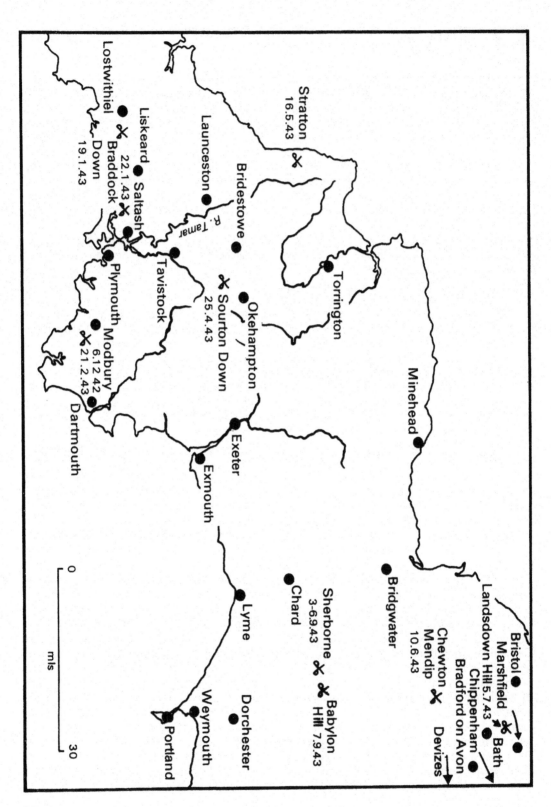

Stratton
16.5.43

Lostwithiel
Braddock
Down
19.1.43

Liskeard
Saltash
22.1.43

Launceston

Bridestowe

R. Tamar

Torrington

Tavistock

Okehampton

Sourton Down
25.4.43

Plymouth Modbury
6.12 42
21.2.43

Dartmouth

Exeter

Exmouth

Minehead

Bridgwater

Chard

Sherborne
3.6.43

Babylon
Hill 7.9.43

Lyme

Dorchester

Weymouth

Portland

Bristol
Marshfield
Landsdown Hill 5.7.43
Chippenham
Bath
Bradford on Avon
Chewton
Mendip
10.6.43
Devizes

0

mls

30

MAP 10 1642–1643: War in the West

The marquess of Hertford, the King's commander in the West, had been active in Somerset since the end of July 1642, but early in August parliamentarian pressure obliged him to concentrate at Sherborne, where he recruited and waited upon events. A desultory siege was laid to the town by the earl of Bedford's forces on 3 September, but the cavaliers were too eager for the earl, who first tried to talk his way out, and then marched precipitately away, under constant attack, on 6 September. The royalist defeat at Babylon Hill on the 7th briefly halted their momentum. Hertford withdrew towards Bristol, but disputes in the royalist command split the army, the marquess moving away to join the King, and Hopton taking a smaller force into Cornwall. Bedford, confident all was contained, likewise gave up and went to rejoin the earl of Essex. Hopton's arrival in Cornwall on 25 September, however, gave the local royalists impetus, and they took Launceston and held the Tamar, looking across into Devon. Hopton planned to assault Plymouth, but he needed Devonshire men, and a conjunction was thwarted at Modbury on 6 December by the parliamentary commander, Ruthin. Hopton turned against Exeter, but was again out-manoeuvred by Ruthin who secured the city, causing the royalists to fall back. Unable to cross the Tamar, Ruthin waited for reinforcements under the earl of Stamford, but these proving dilatory, he advanced and occupied Liskeard. Hopton rallied, routed Ruthin at Braddock Down on 19 January 1643, and took Liskeard. Cornwall secured, the royalists advanced again into Devon, stormed Saltash on 22 January, and prepared to blockade Plymouth. The parliamentarians rallied, took Modbury on 21 February, and obliged Hopton to draw his army together and retreat on Tavistock. A forty day truce was then concluded, by which Hopton at least hoped to take some advantage. Lord Stamford and the main parliamentary army lay at Exeter when, on 22 April, the truce ended and a contingent advanced on Launceston. An inconclusive action at Beacon Hill nearby preceded the battle of Sourton Down on 25 April where the royalists were heavily defeated and forced to fall back on Bridestowe.

Captured letters revealed royalist plans to join Prince Maurice in Somerset, and the earl of Stamford ordered a general rendezvous at Torrington prior to advancing into Cornwall to settle with Hopton once and for all.

The engagement that followed, the battle of Stratton fought on 16 May, was crucial for the Cornish royalists, and Hopton's tactical genius secured a sweeping victory. Launceston was occupied, and Hopton advanced to Chard in Somerset to join Prince Maurice and Hertford on 4 June, leaving Plymouth and Exeter partially blockaded. This sizeable royalist force was ostensibly under Hertford's command, but he lacked the skill of Hopton and Maurice, the latter having already dealt with their new adversary, Waller, at Ripple Field. Waller lay about Bath, and the royalists moved against him, the fight at Chewton Mendip on 10 June ushering in their appearance at Bradford on Avon six miles from the city on 2 July. On 3 July Hopton and Maurice advanced, driving Waller's forces back on Bath, but the royalist force was in two bodies, and Waller had time to draw up in position on Lansdown Hill, an easily defended promontory. The royalists fell back to Marshfield, but on 5 July they moved to engage Waller. After initial hesitancy, which Waller sought to capitalise on, the royalists drew up in the afternoon at the foot of Lansdown Hill and attempted to storm it, but were repeatedly driven back until Sir Bevil Grenville and his Cornishmen made a vigorous charge and withstood all attempts to dislodge them. Grenville himself was killed. The royalist cavalry had broken, however, and only Waller's decision to disengage saved the royalist army from itself retreating in disorder. Hopton's own wounds, caused by exploding powder, incapacitated him and the royalist army, in a demoralised state, retreated to Marshfield and Chippenham, entering Devizes on 9 July. Sir William Waller, anticipating a more sweeping victory, pursued them, and appeared before Devizes as the royalist rearguard entered the town. Prince Maurice commanded the army to be drawn up for battle on Roundway Hill.

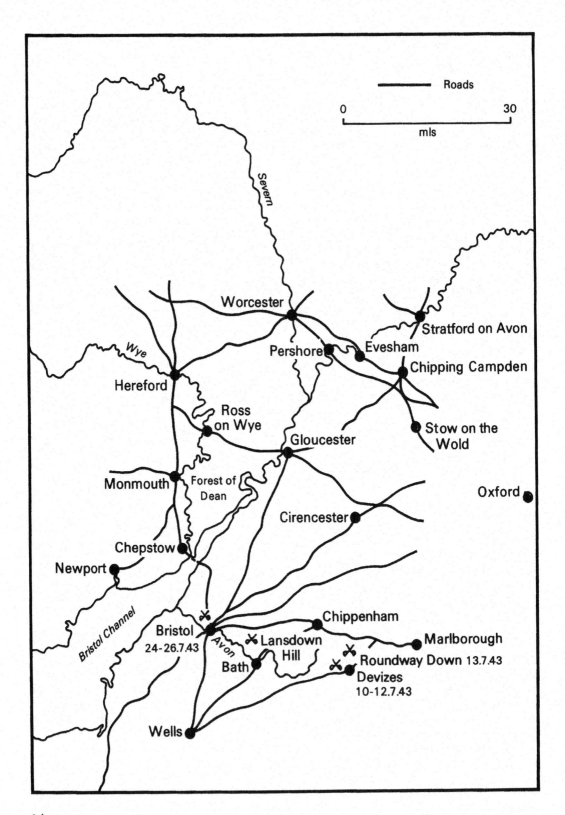

MAP 11 1643: Roundway Down and the Fall of Bristol

On 10 July Sir William Waller, having pursued the royalists to Devizes, faced them drawn up on Roundway Hill, but Prince Maurice abandoned his position and withdrew into the town. Waller moved forward and established his army to the north. The royalist commanders decided to split their army, sending the horse to Oxford, whilst the wounded Hopton held Devizes with the foot. Prince Maurice moved rapidly, entering Oxford on 11 July after a night march, to find reinforcements already on their way west. Whilst Waller bombarded Devizes, the royalist cavalry returned under Henry Wilmot, the intention being to synchronise an attack on Waller by relief forces and garrison. Advised of Wilmot's approach, Waller drew off from the siege, but the garrison commanders declined to march out in pursuit of him, thus obliging Wilmot to face 4,500 parliamentary troops with a mere 1,800 of his own. The parliamentarians marched onto Roundway Down, Sir Arthur Hesilrige's 'impenetrable' regiment on the right wing of cavalry. After initial skirmishing, Wilmot charged, and Hesilrige, who blocked his own cannon's line of fire, saw his famous regiment broken and outflanked. The parliamentarian cavalry abandoned the field in large numbers, leaving the foot to fight it out. Within Devizes, Hopton finally overcame the reluctance of his fellow commanders, and the Cornish infantry left the town to join the action on the Down. The parliamentary foot were broken up, and Waller's potentially fine army had been destroyed. The royalist cavalry had again proved their worth.

Two days after the battle, on 15 July, Prince Rupert left Oxford to reinforce the western army, which had occupied Bath, although Wilmot had returned to Oxford. Waller fled to Gloucester and so made his way back to London to report his 'dismal defeat'. Under Rupert, the western army moved on Bristol, a crucial port giving access to Ireland, and the city was summoned to surrender on 24 July. Nathaniel Fiennes, the commander, refused, trusting in his formidable fortifications and the disposition of his numerous pieces of artillery. Rupert ordered a storm, although some of the western army were reluctant to commit their men to such an audacious and probably costly venture which might not succeed. The date was fixed for 26 July, the initial assault to go in at dawn, but the Cornishmen facing Temple Gate went in too early, and the storm began prematurely as a consequence.

The royalists were beaten off with heavy losses from Priors Hill Fort, and their commander, Grandison, killed, whilst the attempt on Windmill Hill failed for want of ladders to scale the walls. The sector of wall between Windmill Hill and Brandon Hill, however, was carried by a determined assault, and the royalists broke through, pulling down the defences with their bare hands. The defending infantry were paralysed with indecision, and a cavalry charge failed to dislodge the royalists who were steadily being reinforced. Elsewhere, the Cornish foot suffered heavy losses, particularly in officers, but failed to make any impact on their sector of the defences. By mid-afternoon only the initially successful attackers were within the defences, but they made good ground after reinforcement with cavalry. Forced to a stand at Frome Gate for about two hours, the royalists finally broke through despite heavy casualties and began to infiltrate amongst the houses. Fiennes, the governor, sent an offer to surrender to Rupert to forestall any further loss of blood, and marched out with his garrison. In London he faced court-martial and was barely saved from execution by political influence. The fall of Bristol was a serious blow to the Parliament, and it seemed as if the South-West was going to fall effortlessly into royalist hands. Dorchester, Weymouth and Portland fell and Dorset was overrun, with the exception of Lyme. Prince Maurice and the western army moved off to deal with Exeter and Plymouth.

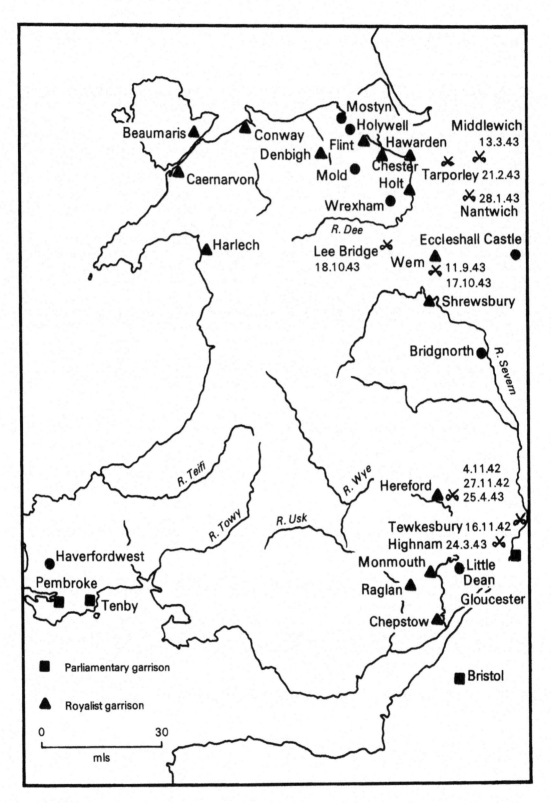

Beaumaris
Conway
Mostyn
Holywell
Middlewich
13.3.43
Flint
Denbigh
Hawarden
Caernarvon
Mold
Chester
Holt
Tarporley 21.2.43
✂ ✂
✂ 28.1.43
Nantwich
Wrexham
R. Dee
Harlech
Lee Bridge ✂
18.10.43
Eccleshall Castle
Wem ✂ 11.9.43
17.10.43
▲ Shrewsbury
Bridgnorth
R. Severn
R. Teifi
R. Wye
4.11.42
27.11.42
Hereford ✂ 25.4.43
R. Towy
R. Usk
Tewkesbury 16.11.42 ✕
Highnam 24.3.43 ✂
Haverfordwest
Monmouth
Little
Dean
Pembroke
Raglan
Gloucester
Tenby
Chepstow
■ Parliamentary garrison
▲ Royalist garrison
0   30
mls
■ Bristol

MAP 12 1642–1643: War in Wales and the Borders

After raising the royal standard at Nottingham, the King marched to Derby where he received word that Shrewsbury was ready to receive him. He reached the town on 20 September, began recruiting there, and established a royal Mint. North Wales was fairly solidly royalist, and contributed largely to the royal army which fought at Edgehill in October, whilst in South Wales the marquess of Worcester and his clients proved diligent in their efforts on the King's behalf, efforts which were enhanced by a visit of Prince Charles to Raglan Castle. On 12 October the King left Shrewsbury and marched to Bridgnorth *en route* to the confrontation with the earl of Essex at Edgehill. In South Wales, the royalists recruited heavily, money being provided by the marquess of Worcester without restraint and on 4 November an army under the marquess of Hertford advanced on Hereford, held by the Parliament. Turning aside, the royalists moved on Tewkesbury, where they were broken by the earl of Stamford on 16 November. The fugitives escaped back into Wales. On 27 November, however, Hertford moved against Hereford once more and, although again beaten, Hereford was abandoned and the county fell into royalist hands. In North Wales, the royalists held firm control, and Chester was a garrison city, so that Wales was protected by a chain of fortified points along its border. Only Pembroke and Tenby remained in Parliamentarian hands, although Chester was threatened by a strong parliamentary party within its county. On 28 January the royalists were routed at Nantwich, which place was then garrisoned and fortified by Sir William Brereton, but Welsh troops poured into Chester itself to strengthen it. On 21 February at Tarporley there was a drawn action, and on 13 March forces from Chester were defeated in an attempt on Middlewich.

From the south of Wales, meanwhile, an attempted advance on Gloucester by royalist forces had been halted with heavy losses in the Forest of Dean, but the advance was pressed and they came to Highnam where Sir William Waller and the Gloucester garrison made short work of them on 24

March. Waller advanced into Wales, taking Chepstow and Monmouth, then turned back for Gloucester, defeating an attempt to stop him at Little Dean. Waller turned on Hereford, summoning it on 25 April and, after a brief storm, the city surrendered. Lord Capel, royalist commander in the north, reported Cheshire quite overrun, and the border country was under severe parliamentarian pressure. On 11 June Sir Thomas Myddleton became Parliament's Major General for North Wales, and a positive parliamentarian campaign was likely. Nevertheless, for most of the summer of 1643 no heavy fighting occurred in Wales or on its borders, the real seat of war being elsewhere in England. Myddleton arrived finally at Nantwich on 10 August, and after an excursion into Staffordshire with Brereton to besiege Eccleshall Castle, the parliamentary army moved into Shropshire and took Wem on 11 September, which became their headquarters and only garrison in the county. In South Wales, however, the royalist earl of Carbery reduced Tenby to obedience and began to muster local forces at Haverfordwest, encountering little or no resistance. With Myddleton and Brereton occupied around Wem, Lord Capel, royalist commander in the north, proposed an attack on Nantwich, failing which, on 17 October, he moved towards Wem but was driven off by a token garrison under Colonel Mytton. On the 18th the retreating royalist army was caught at Lee Bridge on its way to Shrewsbury by Brereton and severely beaten. On 7 November the parliamentary forces left Nantwich and marched on Holt, being reinforced by detachments from Lancashire on their way. Holt town fell, but the castle held, and the parliamentarians went on to take Wrexham, Hawarden, Flint, Mold and Holywell, summoning Denbigh. On 18 November, however, royalist reinforcements from the army in Ireland landed at Mostyn, the parliamentarians retreated and Hawarden came under siege. Myddleton and Brereton abandoned their gains and fell back precipitately on Nantwich, whilst their Cheshire garrisons fell one by one into royalist hands.

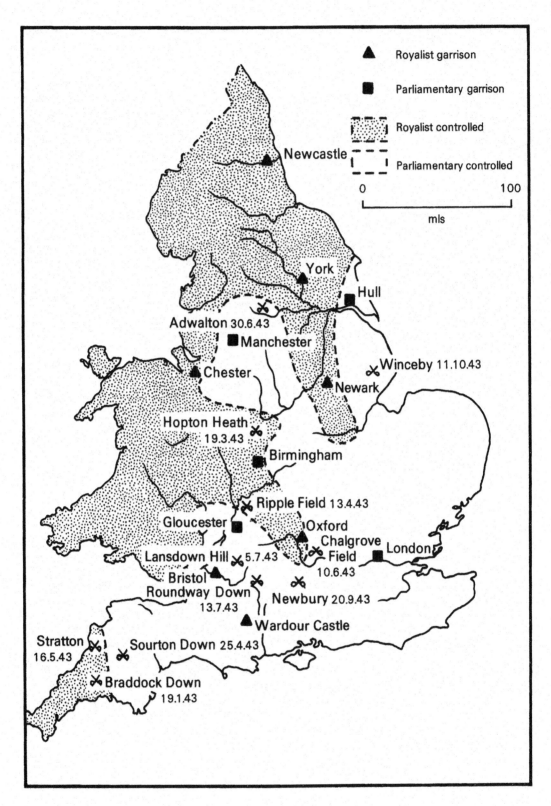

Royalist garrison

Parliamentary garrison

Royalist controlled

Parliamentary controlled

0   100

mls

Newcastle

York

Hull

Adwalton 30.6.43

Manchester

Winceby 11.10.43

Chester

Newark

Hopton Heath
19.3.43

Birmingham

Ripple Field 13.4.43

Gloucester

Oxford

Chalgrove
Field

London

Lansdown Hill 5.7.43

Bristol

Roundway Down
13.7.43

Newbury 20.9.43

10.6.43

Wardour Castle

Stratton
16.5.43

Sourton Down 25.4.43

Braddock Down
19.1.43

MAP 13 The Military Situation in Late 1643

Despite the heavy fighting, albeit somewhat localised, since Edgehill in October 1642, the King's forces, which needed to reach London to bring the war to an effective end, were still very much confined to the north and west of the country; in other words, to their primary recruiting grounds and areas of support. On the other hand, the forces of the parliament had been unable to make headway of any enduring nature, and rested content with acting on a largely defensive basis. The most successful royalist army had undoubtedly been that of the earl of Newcastle operating out of Yorkshire, which, after a tedious lull induced by need to protect the person of the Queen on her way to Oxford, had launched a major offensive in the early summer. Adwalton Moor (30 June) broke the back of parliamentary field forces in the north, and the eastern seaboard lay open to an advance on London in conjunction with the King's armies in the west. Whether or not this was a practical strategic objective, it did not materialise, the successes of the northern army being frittered away in a pointless siege of Hull. Although Lancashire appeared to be under parliamentary control, this was largely due to the lack of a real royalist presence in the county, and apart from incursions into Yorkshire and Cheshire, the commanders at Manchester were content to hold their own and bother no one. In the east, the parliamentary forces were constantly threatened by the powerful royalist garrison at Newark on Trent which they were unable to reduce or even seriously to challenge. Parliamentary control of much of northern Lincolnshire proved tenuous, and was always liable to evaporate under a determined push from Yorkshire by Newcastle's forces. Only when Newcastle was preoccupied at Hull was the Eastern Association able to win a convincing victory, at Winceby in October. In the Midlands, the fighting was relatively frequent, since the area came directly under the eyes of the King and his advisers at Oxford. Hopton Heath was a costly royalist victory (19 March) and led to Prince Rupert's intervention to secure a precarious control in the Birmingham area. The parliamentary generals, Essex and Waller, ably assisted by Massey from Gloucester garrison, were a constant thorn in royalist flesh, and the victory at Ripple Field (13 April) was a necessary boost for royalist morale. A second royalist victory at Chalgrove Field was followed up by a fruitless attempt to take Gloucester, inducing the earl of Essex to set off from London to raise the siege. At Newbury (20 September) the King and Essex fought to a standstill, both armies extricating themselves with difficulty, and although the advantage clearly seemed to lie with the royalists, nothing whatever came of it. London lived in fear of an eastwards march that never materialised.

In a sense, the war in western England was almost distinct from that elsewhere. Although Ralph Hopton galvanised massive armed support for the King in Cornwall, and despite his undoubted military ability, he long proved unable to push forward into Devonshire and thus repair the damage sustained by the royalist cause in Somerset and Wiltshire at the end of 1642. Only in June did a concerted royalist presence make itself felt in Somerset, in confrontation with parliamentary forces under Waller which had suffered badly at Ripple Field further north. The royalist victory at Lansdown (5 July) was far too costly and led to a retreat. Roundway Down (13 July) averted disaster thanks to Henry Wilmot's tactical skill, and the reduction of Bristol, giving access to the Irish sea routes, was a crucial royalist success. On balance, the advantage towards the end of 1643 lay with the King: in reality, there was no co-ordinated scheme of following up successes on a broad front. It was probably logistically impossible.

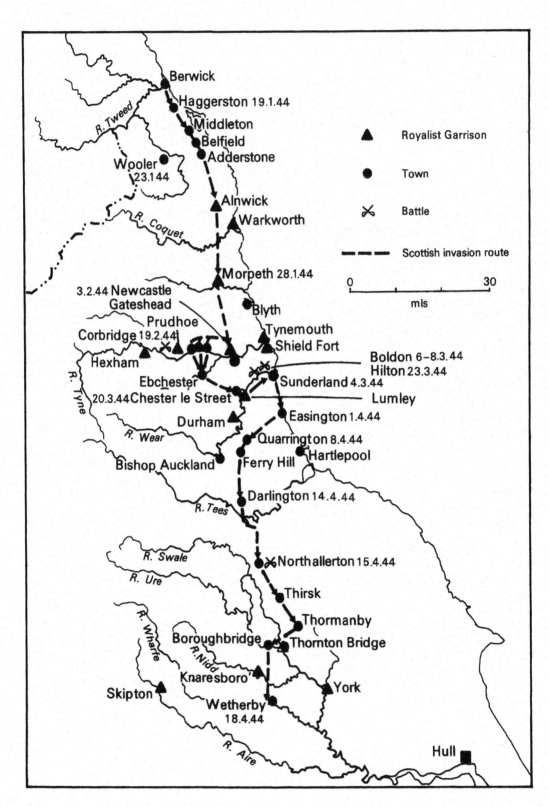

Berwick
Haggerston 19.1.44
Middleton
Belfield
Adderstone
Wooler
23.1.44
R. Tweed
R. Coquet
Alnwick
Warkworth
Morpeth 28.1.44
3.2.44 Newcastle
Gateshead
Blyth
Prudhoe
Tynemouth
Corbridge 19.2.44
Shield Fort
Hexham
Boldon 6–8.3.44
Hilton 23.3.44
Ebchester
Sunderland 4.3.44
20.3.44 Chester le Street
Lumley
Durham
Easington 1.4.44
R. Tyne
R. Wear
Quarrington 8.4.44
Bishop Auckland
Ferry Hill
Hartlepool
Darlington 14.4.44
R. Tees
R. Swale
Northallerton 15.4.44
R. Ure
Thirsk
Thormanby
R. Wharfe
Boroughbridge
Thornton Bridge
R. Nidd
Knaresboro'
York
Skipton
Wetherby
18.4.44
R. Aire
Hull

▲ Royalist Garrison

● Town

✕ Battle

━ ━ ━ Scottish invasion route

0   30

mls

40

MAP 14 War in the North: The Scottish Invasion, January to April 1644

In September 1643 Parliament and the Scots reached an agreement, the Solemn League and Covenant, whereby more than 20,000 Scottish troops would enter the war against the King. Scottish involvement would force the royalists in the north to stand on the defensive and thus ease pressure on Parliament's forces elsewhere in England. The northern royalist army had marked time since its failure to take Hull in September 1643, largely due to command indecision. By January 1644, invasion was imminent, and on the 18th the Scottish army gathered at Berwick. The marquess of Newcastle was faced with war on two fronts, and chose to leave Yorkshire to fend for itself, rightly seeing the Scots as his most immediate enemy.

The earl of Leven, the Scottish commander, was cautious, unwilling to commit his raw forces to a pitched battle with royalist veterans. Nevertheless, he encountered no opposition at all in Northumberland, royalist advance units merely relaying reports back to Newcastle on Tyne, and then burning bridges to hinder the Scottish advance. Sir Thomas Glemham, newly appointed governor of Newcastle, after conferring with local royalists, abandoned Alnwick and burned Aln bridge, consolidating his forces within Newcastle itself. The Scots, at Wooler on 23 January, where they waited upon ammunition being brought across the Tweed, took Morpeth on the 28th. Leven then moved on Newcastle itself where he seems to have expected little resistance. Heavy snow delayed him, however, enabling the marquess of Newcastle to enter the town with his army from Yorkshire only hours before the Scots appeared to the north. Leven's summons to surrender was rejected by Glemham and his new reinforcements, whilst royalist cavalry patrolled the Tyne crossings. Lacking artillery, which did not arrive until 7 February, Leven launched an infantry assault which was repulsed, and on the 8th tried to occupy Gateshead with his cavalry but was driven off. In bitter weather, the Scots slowly consolidated their occupation north of Tyne, but on 19 February a royalist cavalry raid led by Sir Marmaduke Langdale broke up Scottish forces at Corbridge, whilst royalist raiders out of Prudhoe harried enemy lines

of communication. Envisaging a decline in morale unless something positive was achieved, Leven decided to force the crossing of the Tyne, and the bad weather and royalist exhaustion assisted him. Leaving a token force to face Newcastle on Tyne, the Scots drew up along the river from 23 to 28 February, and then crossed at Ovingham, Bywell and Eltringham. Leven then turned east, occupied Sunderland on 4 March and gained access to supplies from the sea. The marquess of Newcastle fell back on Durham with his cavalry and was reinforced from Yorkshire, apparently intending to try to force Leven to a pitched battle. Between 6 and 8 March the armies manoeuvred around the Boldon Hills following a royalist advance on Sunderland, but Leven kept his distance and bad weather hampered the royalist cavalry, as did lack of fodder for the horses. The royalist army fell back on Durham, Leven appeared to follow, then retired on Sunderland. On 20 March, the Scots raided Chester le Street, stinging the royalists into a second advance on Sunderland culminating in the indecisive engagement at Hilton on 23 March. Again, Leven held back from committing his army, despite savage skirmishes, and the royalists returned to Durham disheartened. The Scots moved forward to Easington on 1 April, and to Quarrington on the 8th. On 11 or 12 April, the marquess of Newcastle heard reports of the serious defeat sustained by royalist forces in Yorkshire at Selby, and the consequent threat both to York itself and to the royalist lines of communication. Durham was then abandoned, Lumley Castle and Bishop Auckland stripped of their garrisons, and the royalists hastened towards the Tees. Leven, sure of himself now, pursued, entered Darlington on 14 April where he took prisoners, and on the 15th reached Northallerton in Yorkshire where a single royalist infantry regiment offered futile resistance. The main royalist army reached York safely shortly before Leven met the parliamentary commanders in the county at Wetherby on 18 April. The speed of the Scottish advance and the relatively intact state of his army justified Leven's caution. Northumberland and Durham were lost to the royalists, with the exception of Newcastle, and it seemed that York itself would fall.

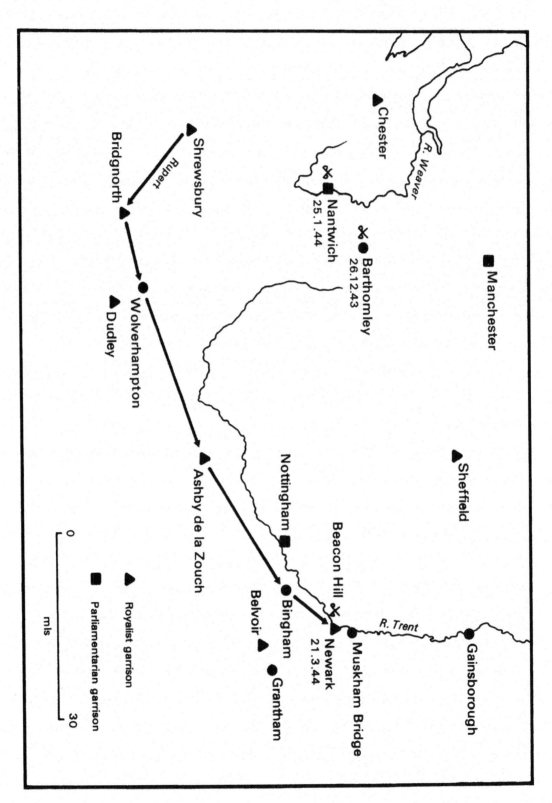

Manchester

Chester

R. Weaver

Nantwich
25.1.44

Barthomley
26.12.43

Sheffield

Shrewsbury

Bridgnorth

Rupert

Dudley

Wolverhampton

Ashby de la Zouch

Nottingham

Beacon Hill

R. Trent

Belvoir

Bingham

Newark
21.3.44

Muskham Bridge

Gainsborough

Grantham

0

30

mls

▲ Royalist garrison

■ Parliamentarian garrison

MAP 15 1644: War in Cheshire and the Relief of Newark

The year 1643 had ended in Cheshire and North Wales with the wholesale retreat of the parliamentary forces into Nantwich, following the arrival in large numbers of royalist reinforcements from the army operating in Ireland, all veterans of the Irish wars. On 26 December John Lord Byron and his forces stormed Barthomley Church and put the entire garrison to the sword, with a ferocity all the more marked for Byron's laconic report of it. Brereton in Nantwich was under terrible pressure, and the Committee of Both Kingdoms in London ordered Sir Thomas Fairfax, then in Lincolnshire, to march to Brereton's aid. The siege of Nantwich had been commenced by Byron on 13 December, but with no great hurry, and the first assault, repulsed, did not go in until 18 January. On 24 January Fairfax, with an army reinforced from Manchester, advanced towards the royalist siege lines from the north-west, driving in a detachment sent to block his road. Byron did not at once draw off from the siege: a sudden thaw caused the River Weaver to flood and Beam Bridge to be broken up and, in consequence, left the royalist infantry without cavalry support to the west of the river. Byron had now to move fast to join up with them, whilst Sir Thomas Fairfax had the chance to tackle the royalist foot piecemeal. The battle of Nantwich, begun on 25 January, at first went in the royalists' favour, but faulty dispositions worked in the interests of Fairfax, and he won a sweeping victory, inflicting heavy losses on Byron's army.

In the wake of it, the royalist command in Oxford ordered Prince Rupert to take overall command of the situation and to repair the damage, and he reached Shrewsbury in early February. His attention, however, was to be deflected from Cheshire by events to the east around the major royalist fortress of Newark on the Trent. This had been left exposed by the defeat at Winceby in the previous October, and the parliamentarians were gathering their strength to take it. The governor, Sir Richard Byron, had no hope of help from the marquess of Newcastle, who was involved with the Scots in Durham, and a powerful siege army under Sir John Meldrum was to be reckoned with. On 6 March Meldrum took Muskham Bridge, but failed in an attempted storm, whilst raiders from Belvoir Castle kept him occupied. Rupert, in Chester on 12 March, was ordered from Oxford to relieve Newark, and he moved rapidly. On the 15th he was at Bridgnorth where troops from Ireland came into him, and on the 16th he was at Wolverhampton where he was reinforced by the governor of Dudley, Thomas Leveson. An attempt by Meldrum to prevent the junction of Rupert with men under Henry Hastings at Ashby de la Zouch on 18 March failed, and on the 20th the royalist army appeared at Bingham within an hour's march of Newark. The royalist army was slightly smaller than Meldrum's, but it was a veteran force, and the parliamentarian commanders were divided as to whether to fight or not. Rupert certainly intended to have a battle, and on 21 March in the darkness of the early morning, he advanced and occupied Beacon Hill. Without waiting for his full army to come into line, the Prince launched an immediate charge, which was well received by the parliamentary horse from Nottinghamshire, but which drove the Lincolnshire cavalry in panic from the field. Rupert himself was in the thick of the fighting and in imminent danger, but his cavalry were unstoppable. Meldrum's remaining forces were surrounded and beyond relief, some of them mutinied, and he was obliged to surrender what was left of his army. The relief of Newark was one of the most significant triumphs of Rupert's career for it showed his abilities as a field commander to advantage, but it was also crucial for the future of the royalist war effort in the Midlands. Newark garrison commanded major strategic routes, and its survival as a constant thorn in the side of the Parliament's war efforts was entirely the result of Prince Rupert's speedy and well executed march and attack.

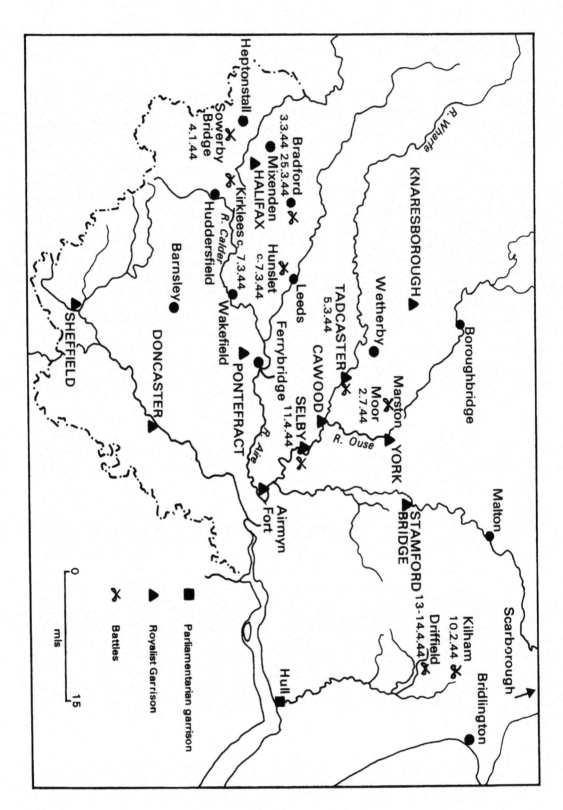

Heptonstall

Sowerby
Bridge
4.1.44

Bradford
3.3.44 25.3.44

Mixenden
HALIFAX

Kirklees c. 7.3.44

R. Calder

Huddersfield

Hunslet
c.7.3.44

Leeds

Wakefield

Barnsley

SHEFFIELD

DONCASTER

PONTEFRACT

Ferrybridge 11.4.44

R. Aire

Airmyn
Fort

SELBY

CAWOOD

TADCASTER
5.3.44

Wetherby

KNARESBOROUGH

R. Wharfe

Marston
Moor
2.7.44

YORK

R. Ouse

Boroughbridge

STAMFORD
BRIDGE 13-14.4.44

Driffield

Kilham
10.2.44

Malton

Scarborough

Bridlington

Hull

Parliamentarian garrison

Royalist Garrison

Battles

mls

0   15

44

MAP 16
War in the North: Fighing in Yorkshire, January to April 1644

The failure to take the garrison port of Hull in the autumn of 1643 had not signalled the progressive collapse of royalist power in Yorkshire. Although the failure boosted parliamentarian morale, it was the invasion of the Scots in January 1644 which gave the Fairfaxes opportunity to exploit consequent weaknesses in royalist military control of the county. When the marquess of Newcastle marched north to face the Scots on 28 January, he left behind a small, basically Yorkshire-raised army commanded by John Belasyse, who was instructed to contain parliamentarian incursions and also to ferry men and supplies northwards to the main army. The inherent problems of Belasyse's task contributed to his defeat at Selby in April.

Parliamentarian infiltration raids from Lancashire were regular events, but of short duration. On 4 January irregulars had raided Sowerby but had been broken up at Mixenden, and their base at Heptonstall had fallen to the royalists. The royalist command post at Halifax was abandoned in late January, however, when Belasyse rationalised his dispositions, intending to rely upon his cavalry to contain the East and West Ridings. There were major garrisons in Sheffield and Doncaster, and at York which was the headquarters of civil and military government. On 10 February, cavalry out of Hull destroyed a royalist contingent at Kilham near Driffield, and on the 12th the raiders took Bridlington. Turning back towards Hull, they won a third success at Driffield, in all cases taking many prisoners. On the 20th, the raiders (perhaps the same body of Hull cavalry) stormed Whitby under the noses of the royalists in Scarborough. Reacting to these niggling reverses, Belasyse redeployed his forces, perhaps stung by a successful attack on Stamford Bridge, near York. Nevertheless, Belasyse was more concerned with the West Riding. He established a command at Leeds, and on 3 March royalist forces clashed with regular parliamentarian troops at Bradford. These, under Major General John Lambert, were fresh from active service in Cheshire, and Lambert intended to disrupt Belasyse's hold on the Riding by swift raids. Bradford fell and was briefly occupied. Tadcaster was taken around 6 March, and at the same time the royalists sustained a defeat at Kirklees and another at Hunslet, the distance between these points indicating the strain on Belasyse's resources.

John Belasyse now put all his efforts into controlling the West Riding. Using York as his administrative base with responsibility for the North Riding and the route into Durham, and establishing troops in Malton to watch the East Riding, he moved his field command to Selby on the River Ouse. He was thus poised between Hull and the forces in the west. Belasyse was probably encouraged in his strategic thinking by Prince Rupert's relief of Newark on 21 March, which ought to have set forces free to reinforce the royalist field army. However, on 25 March or thereabouts (the date is uncertain) Belasyse again marched on Bradford, held by Lambert, and was within an ace of victory when Lambert's men made a determined attempt to break out, scattering the royalists opposed to them. Belasyse fell back on Leeds, and Lambert reoccupied Bradford. From Leeds, the royalists withdrew to Selby, for reasons far from clear. Sir Thomas Fairfax, who had now returned to Yorkshire from Cheshire, and who had been ordered to march into County Durham to assist the Scots there, chose instead to strike at Selby first after meeting his father at Ferrybridge. On 11 April an assault was launched and, although the royalists resisted doggedly, the street fighting went against them. Belasyse was taken, wounded, and the bulk of his infantry spoiled. York now lay wide open to the Fairfaxes, defended by only two city regiments and lacking a governor (Sir Thomas Glemham was then in Newcastle on Tyne). News of the disaster at Selby forced the marquess of Newcastle to abandon his war with the Scots and to retreat rapidly into Yorkshire to ensure control of York itself. The siege of York that followed the conjunction of the Scots with the Fairfaxes at Wetherby, led to Rupert's attempt to relieve the town, and so to the battle on Marston Moor in July.

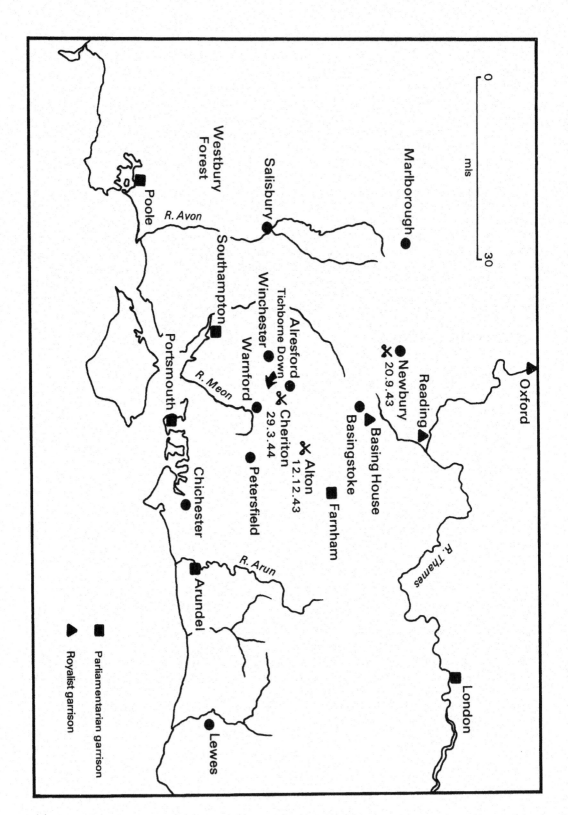

MAP 17 1643–1644: The Fight Against Essex and Waller

After the first battle of Newbury (20 September) the Oxford royalist army occupied Reading, but there was no indication of the major thrust on London. The old western army under Maurice was engaged in Devonshire, the northern army was concerned with Hull. The earl of Essex remained to be dealt with by the Oxford army. It was resolved late in September 1643 at Oxford to create a new western army, the command to be vested in Lord Hopton, arguably the King's best general. This new army was to push towards London through Wiltshire and Hampshire, but at its inception was barely 4,000 strong and inadequate for the task ahead. Hopton's opponent was again to be Waller, commander of a new parliamentarian association of the south-eastern counties. Waller moved first, on 7 November, from his base at Farnham, but was wary of encountering Hopton and instead laid siege to Basing House. Mutiny within his ranks broke the siege up with nothing gained and some losses. He fell back on Farnham. Hopton, reinforced from Oxford and the West Country, detached forces to blockade Portsmouth, Southampton and Poole, and at the end of November advanced against Farnham. Waller refused to face him, and Hopton withdrew, not wishing to waste time in a siege. He put his army into winter-quarters, reduced Arundel Castle, and waited. On 12 December, Waller made his army ready for the march, and set off for his objective, the royalist quarters at Alton.

Alton was garrisoned by horse and foot under Lord Crawford and Richard Bolle with orders to fall back rather than to engage Waller. The parliamentarian army, in excess of 5,000 men, evaded Crawford's watchful cavalry and on 13 December attacked Alton. Crawford abandoned Bolle to his fate and withdrew his cavalry. The royalists drew up around Alton Church, and the ensuing fight was particularly vicious, Bolle refusing to consider surrender even though driven into the church which was partially fortified. The position was hopeless, but Bolle chose to die fighting, and with

him died 700 or more royalist infantry, predominantly veterans. Although a minor engagement, the beating up of a quarter, it was nevertheless taken to heart by Hopton, whose orders to push on to London were becoming more and more difficult to fulfil.

On 6 January Waller took Arundel Castle, and then chose to go into winter-quarters himself. Hopton's lack of achievement was mirrored north of the Thames, too, where another efficient army had wasted much time against the earl of Essex. After taking Newport Pagnell, a vital communications link for the Parliament, the royalists abandoned it after three weeks in October 1643. War north of the Thames appeared to be at a standstill in the winter of 1643/4, so much so that when, after Alton, Hopton requested reinforcements from the Oxford army, he was sent, in March 1644, nearly 2,000 men under Lord Forth, who also had seniority over Hopton. The two old generals worked well together, however, whilst Waller, reinforced by troops from Essex's idle army, now had an army of at least 8,000 men, still considerably outnumbering the royalists. The inevitable confrontation between Hopton and Waller drew nearer, particularly when Hopton began to receive regiments from Ireland into his army. Waller was moving on Winchester, and occupying the Meon Valley, when Hopton moved against him on 26 March 1644. On the 27th, Hopton occupied Warnford, from which the parliamentarians had retreated to Westbury Forest, but attempts to draw Waller into action caused the latter to make for Alresford rather than engage. Hopton's cavalry raced Waller to the town and beat him to it, and proceeded to fortify it as best they could, whilst the parliamentarian army came to rest on Tichborne Down on 27 March. For a day the armies faced each other, Lord Forth retiring to Alresford through ill-health, leaving Hopton to deal with his old adversary, Waller. The battle of Cheriton was fought on 29 March.

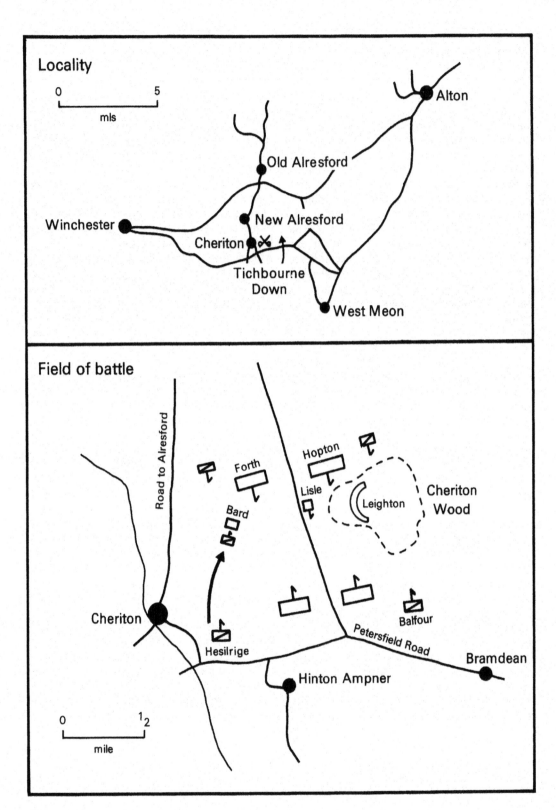

Locality

0   5

mls

Alton

Old Alresford

New Alresford

Winchester

Cheriton

Tichbourne
Down

West Meon

Field of battle

Road to Alresford

Forth

Hopton

Lisle

Cheriton
Wood

Bard

Leighton

Cheriton

Balfour

Hesilrige

Petersfield Road

Bramdean

Hinton Ampner

0   1 2

mile

MAPS 18 & 19 The Battle of Cheriton, 29 March 1644

Hopton's cavalry under Sir Edward Stawell had outpaced Waller's under Balfour, and reached Alresford before the parliamentary army could do so. The long awaited pitched battle seemed to be coming, but on 28 March the parliamentary commanders at Hinton Ampner were divided. Recognising that retreat, however, was as perilous as staying to fight, Waller prepared for action on the 29th. Whilst there is no doubt that Hopton wanted a battle, he was probably surprised to find Waller apparently determined also, and sent word to Lord Forth, who quit Alresford and ordered the royalist army to form up.

Waller occupied Cheriton Wood, threatening the royalist advance position held by Sir George Lisle and forcing a tactical withdrawal. The Wood, however, continued to be a major threat to Hopton's left flank, and he sent Colonel Appleyard with 1,000 musketeers to storm the place: despite fierce resistance from within the Wood, Appleyard, supported by royalist artillery to the north, stormed into the enemy positions and drove the parliamentarian commander, Leighton, to flight. This success gave the royalists control of the high ground, and put the onus upon Waller to force a battle. However, it seems that field commanders on the royalist right wing were unwilling to stand and wait, and after a little while engaged the enemy opposed to them. Henry Bard's regiment, the culprits in this, found themselves hemmed in by Hesilrige's cavalry between the two armies, and were utterly broken. The advantage had slipped again to Waller, who immediately assaulted the royalist infantry facing Balfour's cavalry. The infantry stood their ground, however, despite heavy pressure, and events elsewhere were taking shape. Lord Forth, after Hesilrige's breaking of Bard's regiment, determined to tackle him and, at about two in the afternoon, Sir Edward Stawell advanced to the attack. Despite pressing the attack home, however, Stawell was forced to withdraw without achieving anything, and was himself taken prisoner, badly wounded. Forth sent in the remainder of his cavalry to back up Stawell's men, and the battle then turned into a general conflict.

Hesilrige's heavily armoured cavalry proved too impenetrable an obstacle for the royalist horse, who tried to press home their attack for more than two hours, losing numerous senior officers in the hand-to-hand fighting. Hopton was obliged to cover the cavalry's withdrawal, whilst parliamentarian foot fought their way onto both ends of the ridge. The royalist army fell back on Alresford and drew up to its south; then Hopton and Forth resolved to march off towards Basing House, passing through Alresford *en route*, a manoeuvre that was executed without hindrance from Waller. The army reached Basing on the morning of 30 March, and then proceeded to Reading, which was abandoned when Hopton and Forth returned to the main Oxford army, on direct orders from the King. Waller, meanwhile, was content to reduce Winchester on 30 March, although the royalist garrison in the castle remained obdurate. The battle of Cheriton was a muddled, indecisive affair, the primary results of which were, for the royalists, the loss of too many experienced cavalry commanders and, for the parliamentarians, the confirmation that on their day, their cavalry were the equal of the King's. If the projected royalist advance on London had, indeed, been seriously planned for and considered, it was demonstrably at an end, for Hopton's new western army had ceased to be a distinct and viable unit, whilst Newcastle's army in the north was occupied with the Scots and facing imminent catastrophe in Yorkshire. The year 1644 had started badly for the King.

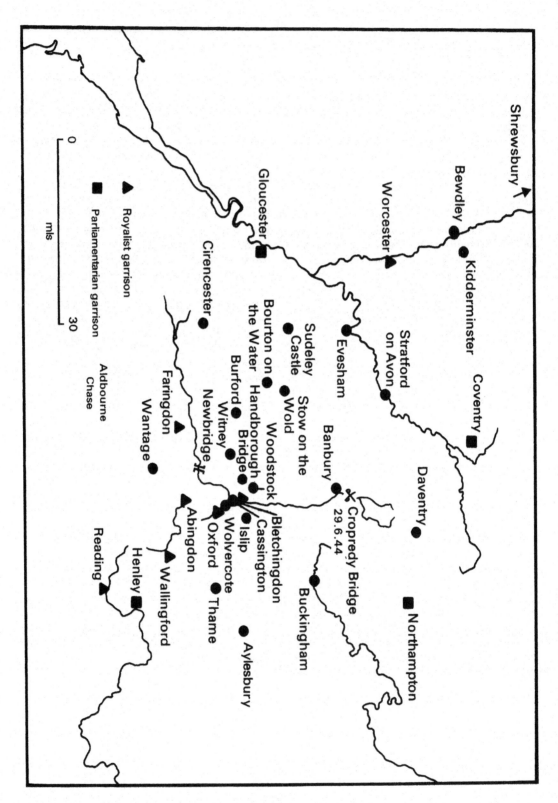

Shrewsbury

Bewdley

Kidderminster

Coventry

Worcester

Gloucester

Cirencester

Bourton on
the Water

Sudeley
Castle

Stow on the
Wold

Evesham

Stratford
on Avon

Banbury

Daventry

Northampton

Buckingham

Cropredy Bridge
29.6.44

Bletchingdon
Cassington

Islip

Wolvercote

Oxford

Thame

Aylesbury

Woodstock

Handborough
Bridge

Witney

Burford

Newbridge

Faringdon

Wantage

Abingdon

Wallingford

Henley

Reading

Aldbourne
Chase

Parliamentarian garrison

Royalist garrison

mls

0   30

50

MAP 20 1644: The Campaigns of the Oxford Army, to July

By the spring of 1644 the royalists were in an unenviable position. The military advantage had swung decidedly in favour of the Parliament and of its Scottish allies, whilst the reinforcements coming from Ireland had proved a mere trickle. There was no real prospect of an alliance with the Irish confederacy. The King, to create a strong enough main army based on Oxford, Reading, Abingdon, Wallingford, Banbury and Faringdon, had taken Hopton's independent force under his own command, and the original western army under Prince Maurice was occupied around Lyme. Parliament now took the initiative, sending Waller against Maurice, and ordering the earls of Manchester and Essex to join together at Aylesbury. Neither of the earls was hopeful of this strategy, and the rendezvous never took place, Manchester certainly regarding the east as vulnerable after Rupert's relief of Newark in March. Waller also advanced no further. On 10 April, the King reviewed his army, 9,000 strong, on Aldbourne Chase, and sent his Queen to safety at Exeter. Prince Rupert came to Oxford on 25 April, and it was resolved to adopt a defensive posture around Oxford whilst Rupert and his brother Maurice dealt with the northern and western theatres respectively. However, the King took further advice, abandoned Reading on 18 May, drew its infantry into his main army, and sent it off to Wantage.

On 17 April Essex's army came to Henley on Thames, where he conferred with Waller, and occupied Reading. On 26 May Essex took Abingdon which had also been abandoned, and the threat to Oxford increased. The royalists determined to wait until Essex and Waller divided, and then tackle each in turn, and so the royal army was concentrated north of Oxford and across the Thames around Cassington. Essex also crossed the Thames and made for Islip. On 1 June Waller's army seized the crossing of the Thames at Newbridge, having marched up from Abingdon, and so serious was this that the King's advisers in Oxford briefly countenanced the idea of surrender. Instead, the King took command of the situation, and sent forces towards Abingdon, inducing Waller to abandon Newbridge. On 3 June, the King at its head, the royalist army marched via Wolvercote and Handborough Bridge to arrive at Bourton-on-the-Water on the 4th. Oxford was garrisoned with 3,000 or so infantry.

Keeping ahead of Essex and Waller, the King reached Worcester on the 6th, when the hoped-for happened. Essex and Waller parted company in acrimony, the earl heading west to tackle Maurice, leaving Waller to face the King alone. From London, frantic orders went out to force Essex to return, but it was too late. The parliamentarian commanders had played into the King's hands and his resolution had proved justified. Waller could do no other than stick to the King. He took Sudeley Castle on 10 June and marched to Evesham, the King left Worcester and made for Bewdley, giving Waller the impression that the royalists intended to make for Shrewsbury. Instead, the royal army back-tracked, entered Worcester on the 15th, and then went on through Evesham to Witney, where the Oxford garrison joined them, and so marched to Buckingham. Waller was at Gloucester on 20 June where he received frantic orders from London to prevent the King from attacking the eastern counties, and he set off towards Banbury, coming near the town on 28 June. The King turned to meet him. Waller's position on Crouch Hill was too strong, however, and the royalists moved towards Daventry to try to create a better opportunity. Waller marched on a parallel course, and the King approached Cropredy township, his army strung out badly as he tried to control the Cherwell crossings. Waller attacked, seizing Cropredy Bridge and Slat Mill ford to its south, and crossed in rear of the King's army. The royalist rearguard counter-attacked at Cropredy, the King turned his army, and Waller was savagely repulsed. The battle of Cropredy Bridge on 29 June was a victory for the King, but he withdrew towards Evesham by 3 July, and then headed west to tackle Essex. Waller's army was totally disrupted and no longer a threat.

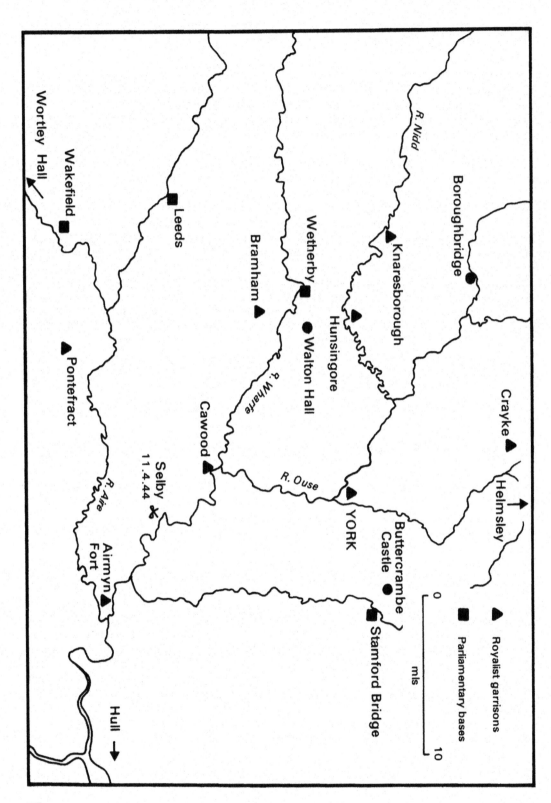

Wortley Hall

Wakefield

Leeds

Bramham

Wetherby

Knaresborough

Boroughbridge

R. Nidd

Pontefract

Hunsingore

Walton Hall

Crayke

Helmsley

R. Aire

Airmyn Fort

Selby
11.4.44

Cawood

R. Wharfe

R. Ouse

YORK

Buttercrambe Castle

Stamford Bridge

Hull

▲ Royalist garrisons

■ Parliamentary bases

0   mls   10

MAP 21 1644: The Siege of York and War in the North-East

The marquess of Newcastle entered York in the wake of the battle of Selby on 11 April, and at once sent away his cavalry to be of use elsewhere. The royalists in Yorkshire and the North-East were on the defensive and in desperate need of relief, although it was unlikely that York itself would fall to the army of the Scots and their Fairfax allies. The siege was not yet particularly close to York itself, and matters elsewhere had to be dealt with. On 24 April the allies took Stamford Bridge, whilst their cavalry watched the movements of Newcastle's cavalry west of York. Cawood Castle repulsed two attacks by the siege army. Much depended on the Scots, whose lines of communication were threatened when, on 10 May, royalist troops under the marquess of Montrose and Robert Clavering recaptured Morpeth Castle in Northumberland and seemed to threaten the Scottish siege forces outside Newcastle upon Tyne. Lumley Castle in Durham was re-garrisoned, and a skirmish was fought near Hexham. By 15 May, Montrose was making headway against the Scots around Newcastle, and 1,000 cavalry were detached from the siege of York to go north. Montrose retired into Newcastle.

On 16 May Buttercrambe Castle fell to the allies, and on the 19th Cawood was finally taken by Sir John Meldrum. Crayke surrendered shortly afterwards, but royalists raiding from Pontefract repeatedly threatened the security of the area south of York. From Cawood, Meldrum went on to take a royalist fort at Airmyn at the junction of the Ouse and Aire rivers, 'one of ye strongest places in England' it was said. On 27 May Bramham Hall near Boston Spa fell to Scottish troops. On the night of 3/4 June, Sir Hugh Cholmeley at Scarborough sent out his raiders to unsettle the allied garrison at Buttercrambe. They drove off the soldiers, who panicked and captured a Parliamentary Commissioner, Henry Darley, whose task was one of constant liaison with the Scottish forces.

Nevertheless, the tide was running against the royalists. An unknown manor near Barnsley fell at the end of May, Wortley Hall capitulated soon after, and on 3 June Walton Hall yielded after initial storm. On 17 June Mulgrave Castle in the North Riding capitulated. Most of these garrisons had been set up, probably in the wake of the battle of Selby, for reasons of local security rather than as part of any major tactical or strategic thinking, and their collapse was not, apart from that of Airmyn, crucial to the defence of York itself. Scarborough, Skipton, Pontefract and Sheffield were more likely to hold out, and were not tackled at all by the allies. Neither was Helmsley, north of York.

The earl of Manchester and the army of the Eastern Association had been ordered to join the siege before York to encompass the city tightly, but he moved slowly, conscious of the threat to the eastern counties from the Oxford army, and only reached the siege lines around York on 27 May, still well ahead of his army, which remained at Selby until 1 June. Now, however, batteries were erected, fortified points constructed, and the work of siege warfare properly begun. Mining was attempted, and St Mary's tower partially demolished, but an attempt to break into the environs of St Mary's Abbey was repulsed in bitter fighting by the royalist garrison, although the royalist commander there, Philip Byron, was killed outright. Outlying redoubts fell to the allies, but they could make no impression on the walls of York itself, where the marquess of Newcastle and his governor, the reliable Sir Thomas Glemham, kept firm control. The siege dragged on through June, the marquess sending frequently to Oxford and to Prince Rupert for relief, and the two sides fraternising regularly. Towards the end of June, however, as Sir Henry Slingsby, a royalist commander, commented, 'he whom we so long look'd for was heard of coming to our relief'. Rupert was at hand.

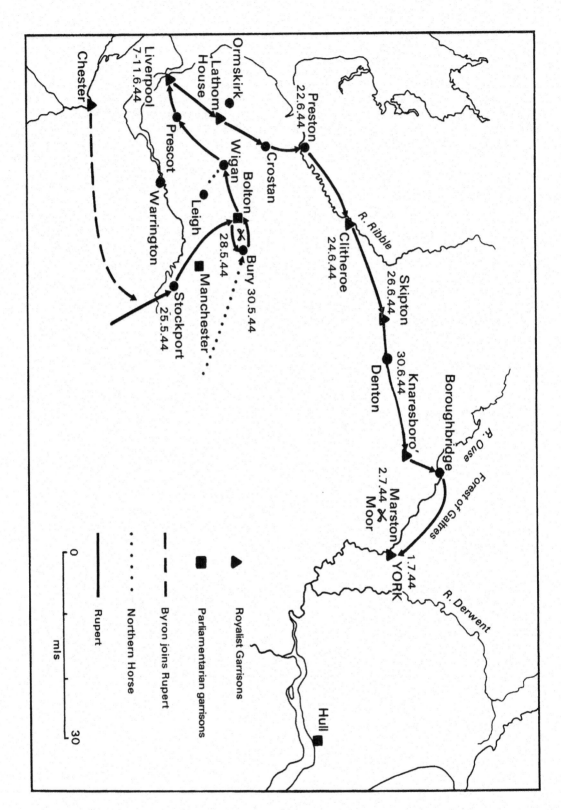

Chester

Ormskirk
Lathom
House

Liverpool
7-11.6.44

Prescot

Warrington

Preston
22.6.44

Crostan

Wigan

Bolton

Leigh

Bury 30.5.44

28.5.44

Manchester

Stockport
25.5.44

R. Ribble

Clitheroe
24.6.44

Skipton
26.6.44

Denton

Knaresboro'
30.6.44

Boroughbridge

R. Ouse

Forest of Galtres

Marston
Moor
2.7.44

YORK
1.7.44

R. Derwent

Hull

Byron joins Rupert

Parliamentarian garrisons

Royalist Garrisons

Rupert

Northern Horse

0   mls   30

MAP 22

After the success of his relief march to Newark (21 March) Prince Rupert retired to Shrewsbury to consolidate his forces. Pleas for help from the marquess of Newcastle against the Scots were frequent, but from mid-April the situation in the North-East was critical. Indecision in the counsels of the King at Oxford delayed assistance for the beleaguered city of York, and Prince Rupert did not finally set off until 16 May. His first objective was to restore royalist control to Lancashire, and there to recruit fresh forces. On 25 May he took Stockport, and the parliamentary commanders in Lancashire panicked. The siege of Lathom House, held for the King by the Countess of Derby, was abandoned after twelve months' ineffectual efforts, and the parliamentary troops fell back on urban garrisons. On 28 May, Bolton was taken by storm, and on the 30th Prince Rupert was reinforced by the marquess of Newcastle's roving cavalry, the Northern Horse, under George Goring. The army advanced on Liverpool via Wigan, appearing before the port on 7 June. After initial resistance, the parliamentary governor fled by sea and the town fell on 11 June. After creating a garrison of local royalists, Rupert ordered extensive fortification works to be begun to keep the port and its Irish Sea contacts secure. Between 11 and 19 June, Rupert marked time in the Liverpool/Lathom House area, but on the 20th marched off towards Preston which he reached on 22 June. Two days later, royalist troops occupied Clitheroe Castle under one of Rupert's closest confidants, Thomas Daniel.

The advance on York was now under way, although the period after the capture of Liverpool had been marked by doubts as to whether it was practicable or not. Letters had passed between the King and his nephew indicating a want of supplies on Rupert's part and a sense of urgency on the King's. Once Clitheroe was occupied, however, Rupert set off rapidly, entering Skipton Castle in Yorkshire, a powerful royalist garrison under Sir John Mallory, on 26 June. 'Wee stayed at Skipton

to fixe our armes, and send into Yorke' wrote the diarist of the march. It is clear, therefore, that the York garrison expected Rupert's imminent arrival. No steps had been taken during his march through Lancashire to impede him seriously, although the parliamentary commander in Manchester, Sir John Meldrum, had repeatedly tried to bring this about by drawing forces into the county to assist him. Rupert's opponents appeared mesmerised. Flowers strewn across the streets of Wigan on 5 June had symbolised too well the widespread latent royalism in Lancashire, and the pressed troops of the parliamentary army there could not be relied upon to face so dangerous an enemy. This fear communicated itself to the allied commanders before York as Rupert drew closer to his objective. On 29 June he occupied a Fairfax mansion at Denton near to Leeds, and on the 30th he was at Knaresborough, another royalist garrison town. The allied commanders expected the Prince to advance on York on the south bank of the Ouse, but instead he swung north towards Boroughbridge and, on the night of 1 July, he lay to the north-west of the city in the Forest of Galtres, whilst he sought to co-ordinate plans with the marquess of Newcastle for pursuit of the allied siege army which had drawn off from the city and lay to its west. The allied generals — Leven, Fairfax and Manchester — were anxious both not to be trapped between Rupert and the garrison, and not to bring about a battle. The marquess of Newcastle was keen to let them get away, believing their allied army would soon disperse, but Rupert was determined to break them at one blow if he could. The Prince's determination and senior authority carried the day, not without misgivings on the part of Newcastle's advisers, and the Prince set off in pursuit of the enemy on the morning of 2 July. The battle that ensued, fought on Hessay or Marston Moor a few miles from York, was perhaps the single most bloody action of the civil war and proved to be a close thing.

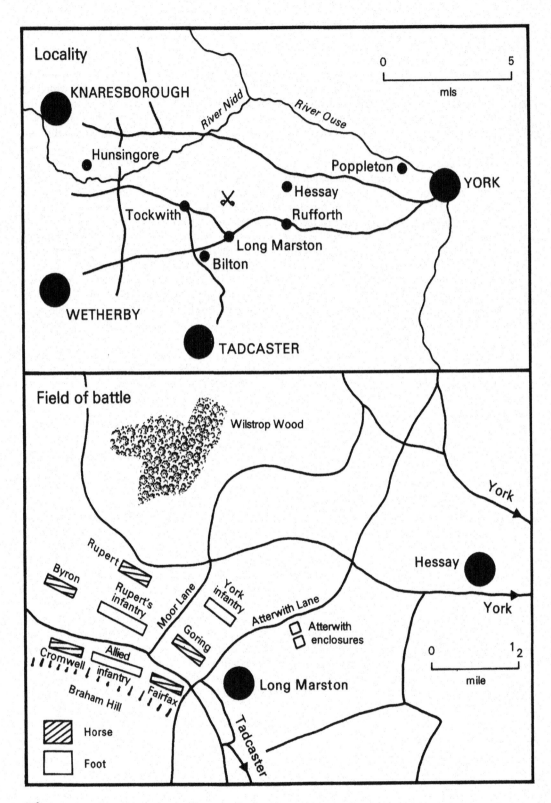

Locality

KNARESBOROUGH

Hunsingore

River Nidd

River Ouse

Poppleton

YORK

Hessay

Tockwith

Rufforth

Long Marston

Bilton

WETHERBY

TADCASTER

0   5
mls

Field of battle

Wilstrop Wood

York

Byron

Rupert

Rupert's infantry

Moor Lane

York infantry

Atterwith Lane

Hessay

York

Goring

Atterwith enclosures

Cromwell

Allied infantry

Braham Hill

Fairfax

Long Marston

Tadcaster

0   1 2
mile

Horse

Foot

MAPS 23 & 24 The Battle of Marston Moor, 2 July 1644

On the morning of 2 July the allied army which had lain encamped on Marston Moor, began to march away towards Tadcaster and so southwards. The rearguard, commanded by Sir Thomas Fairfax, Oliver Cromwell and David Leslie, was alarmed by the sudden appearance of Rupert's army crossing Hessay Moor towards them, and the allied generals were obliged to turn back and to offer battle rather than be caught in line of march. The allied troops drew up in battle order on Braham Hill, cultivated land overlooking Marston Moor proper to the north. Between nine in the morning and late afternoon the two armies mustered their men into position and waited upon events.

The allied commanders on the ridge had a clear view of Rupert's dispositions on the level moor beyond, and so were soon aware of the relative weakness of the royalist infantry centre. This was due to a clash of opinion between Rupert and James King, Newcastle's chief adviser, who as a consequence remained deliberately in York far beyond the appointed time for his arrival on the moor. When he did put in an appearance, with his York infantry strung out in line of march, even the earl of Leven, chief commander of the allied army, saw the moment to attack had come. The allies moved forward off the Braham Hill, to meet with mixed fortune. In the centre, the outnumbered royalist infantry wavered and then fell back, but held firm thereafter. On the allied left, Oliver Cromwell and David Leslie managed to create chaos amongst Byron's cavalry opposed to them partly due to Byron's premature reaction to their charge. After being held for a while by reserve regiments under Molyneux, the royalist right wing finally broke in flight, and Rupert was unable to halt them. Cromwell and Leslie found themselves in the rear of the royalist army and unopposed. On the allied right, Sir Thomas Fairfax encountered difficult terrain and bitter resistance from George Goring, and his cavalry were shattered and virtually chased off the moor and Braham Hill by the marquess of Newcastle's veteran horse. The

battle now hung on which of the two successful cavalry wings would return to the general engagement first, and this proved to be Cromwell's opportunity to show himself a master of tactical manoeuvre. Wheeling southwards, Cromwell and Leslie began to advance in the rear of George Goring, experiencing a temporary halt when they came under fire from an isolated royalist regiment, the Whitecoats, which had dug in behind the hedges of a small enclosure on the moor. Leaving dragoons to deal with this body of men, Cromwell pushed on, striking the rear of the royalist infantry centre in the process, and coming to grips with Goring's scattered cavalry units. The royalist cavalry was thus obliged to fight over terrain which Fairfax had found too difficult and, despite giving a good account of themselves, were severely mauled. Many experienced royalist field commanders were killed in this engagement. With the overthrow of the royalist left wing, therefore, the royalist infantry were progressively fought to a standstill, and the victory, long in the balance, went to the allies. Leven and Lord Fairfax, who had fled as far and as fast as they could when Goring broke onto the Braham Hill, were sent for to return, and the allied army set to work stripping the 4,000 or so dead and dying. Prince Rupert had escaped into York, and so had the marquess of Newcastle, despite his courageous personal showing in the battle, but the army of the north had been virtually destroyed, the remnants of the Northern Horse only remaining intact. These Rupert took with him when he began his march back into Lancashire on 3 July. The marquess of Newcastle and his staff abandoned the city of York, were escorted to Scarborough, and there took ship for Hamburg and exile. The city of York was left to fend for itself, and surrendered on terms on 16 July, Sir Thomas Glemham marching away to continue the war elsewhere. For the Parliament and its allies the turning point of the war had come, for the northern royalist army was finished, and it remained to concentrate on those in the south of the country.

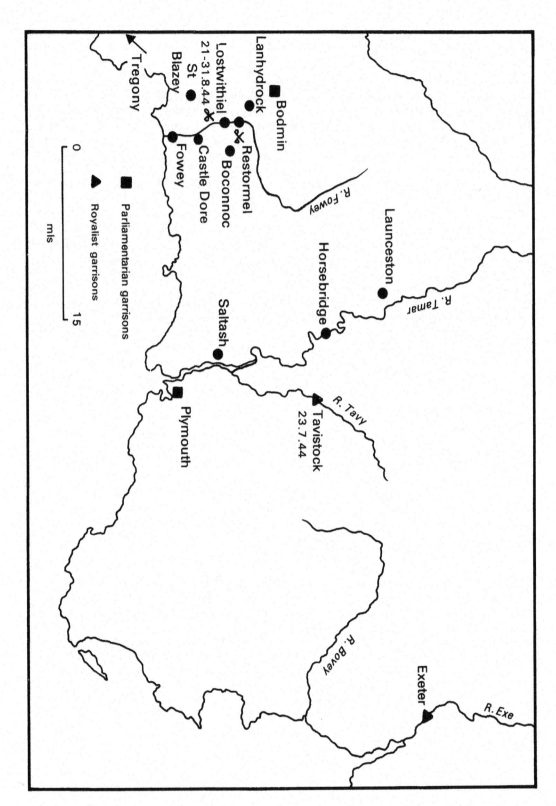

Tregony

Lanhydrock

Bodmin

Lostwithiel
21-31.8.44

St
Blazey

Restormel

Fowey

Castle Dore

Boconnoc

R. Fowey

Launceston

Horsebridge

R. Tamar

Saltash

R. Tavy

Tavistock
23.7.44

Plymouth

0

mls

15

■ Parliamentarian garrisons

▲ Royalist garrisons

R. Bovey

Exeter

R. Exe

MAP 25

After the division of their armies, the earl of Essex had taken his forces into the West Country to deal with Prince Maurice, leaving Waller to tackle the King's Oxford army, which he failed to do. After Cropredy Bridge, the King moved to Evesham on 3 July preparatory to moving against Essex, and the news of the defeat at Marston Moor probably gave him still stronger motivation. Essex had a head-start, however, and took Tavistock on 23 July causing the siege of Plymouth to be lifted and roy-alist troops under Grenville to fall back on Saltash. Grenville manned the crossing of the Tamar at Horsebridge, and Essex had to determine whether to force it, or try to take on the King's advancing army. Under pressure from local parliamentarians, Essex pushed on into Cornwall. On 26 July the King entered Exeter; on 2 August he was at Launceston. Essex was in a tight corner, and fell back on Lostwithiel, seizing Fowey, and sending fearful letters to London. The Cornish under Grenville were at Tregony ready to advance on Lostwithiel, and the earl of Essex had little hope of beating three royalist armies. The Cornish were intractably pro-royalist and he had no hopes of recruiting more forces from amongst them. All he could hope to do was hold Lostwithiel until help arrived by land or sea.

Holding Fowey, the earl established the bulk of his army on Beacon Hill east of Lostwithiel, and in Restormel Castle to the north. On 11 August the Cornish under Grenville took Bodmin by assault, and on the 12th captured Respryn Bridge north of Lostwithiel, establishing contact with the King. On the 13th Lord Goring, who had recently replaced Wilmot as commander of the royalist cavalry, established strongpoints along the Fowey, whilst Essex remained idle. A relief column head-ing for Lostwithiel was broken at Bridgwater. On 21 August the King resolved to attack Lostwithiel all along the front from Lanhydrock to Boconnoc, the royal command post. Grenville stormed and took Restormel Castle, the Devonshire parliamen-tarians pulling out after token resistance only. The

royalist attack pushed in all of Essex's defences, and brought the royalists onto the high ground overlooking Lostwithiel. On the 26th royalist troops advanced to St Blazey to prevent provisions from sea being landed for the parliamentary army, but this was a mere precaution, since the parlia-mentary fleet was nowhere in sight. The King still hesitated about assaulting Lostwithiel, until intelligence came that Essex intended to break out towards Fowey. On 31 August Essex's cavalry under Balfour broke out, reached Saltash and crossed into Devonshire with few losses. The fault lay in a royalist army of 16,000 covering a 15-mile front, but Balfour's determination carried him through. On the same day, 31 August, royalist infantry marched directly into Lostwithiel whilst Essex carried out his dangerous gamble of reaching Fowey, covered by a small rearguard. The King moved on, forded the Fowey, determined to catch the earl's army which was evidently demoralised and on the run. There was a bitter skirmish at Trebathvey Farm which the royalists won and, late in the afternoon after more fighting, the parlia-mentarians tried to establish themselves on high ground near Castle Dore. They held on to this despite attacks, and prepared for action under Major General Skippon, but the earl of Essex had had enough and took boat downstream towards Plymouth. The army was lost, but its command-ing general could not be risked unnecessarily. On 1 September the parliamentary commanders offered to talk with the King's generals, and on the 2nd they surrendered their entire force. They went via Southampton to Portsmouth, whilst Essex from Plymouth got away to London safely. Plymouth again came under siege from the Cornishmen. The King had won a tremendous victory over his old adversary, and there is no doubt that it was Charles's personal involvement at each stage of the campaign and action which won the day as, indeed, it had been at Cropredy Bridge a few months earlier.

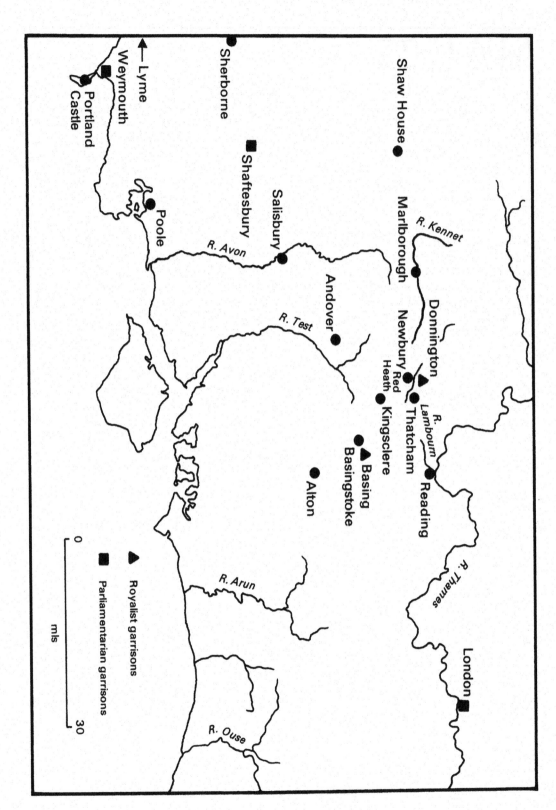

Lyme

Weymouth

Portland
Castle

Sherborne

Shaftesbury

Salisbury

Poole

R. Avon

Andover

R. Test

Marlborough

R. Kennet

Shaw House

Newbury

Donnington

Red
Heath

Kingsclere

Thatcham

R. Lambourn

Reading

Basing

Basingstoke

Alton

R. Arun

R. Thames

London

R. Ouse

Parliamentarian garrisons

Royalist garrisons

mls

0

30

MAP 26 Events Leading to the Second Battle of Newbury

The battle of Lostwithiel, if such it can be called, created grave consternation amongst the parliamentary forces in the Home Counties and to the east. The earl of Manchester's army, fresh from its involvement at Marston Moor and the fall of York, had returned into Lincolnshire when it was ordered to march to the aid of Waller, who lay between the King and an anticipated thrust on London. Manchester was dilatory, disliking his role in the war and resenting the ambition of his inferior, Oliver Cromwell. He got to Reading and moved no further. As it was, the King, having shown himself capable of significant strategic and tactical thinking, now showed himself hesitant again. Leaving forces to besiege Plymouth, he had moved to Exeter, planning to relieve royalist garrisons in Banbury, Basing and Donnington, and showing no awareness of the vulnerable position the overthrow of Essex's army had placed London in. On 2 October he reached Sherborne with an army of 10,000 men, and relieved Portland Castle. Waller was established in Weymouth and Lyme, with his command at Shaftesbury. There was an atmosphere of inactivity after so much movement.

It was decided that Prince Rupert, who had come into Bristol after his dangerous march south following Marston Moor, should take the field to distract at least one of the armies opposing the King. He and Lord Hopton retired to Bristol to prepare for the operation on 5 October. Ten days later, the King's army itself moved, advancing to Salisbury. At once, the earl of Manchester quit Reading and moved into Hampshire, whilst Waller abandoned his positions and retired on Andover to await reinforcements. On 18 October George Goring and his cavalry attacked Andover and forced Waller to quit the town. He joined with the earl of Manchester's army at Basingstoke on the 19th, and on the 20th the remnants of Essex's infantry under Skippon came to Alton. The King's objective was the relief of Basing House, and the united parliamentary armies stood clear in his way. On the 21st, the King reached Kingsclere, only to give up the idea of relief, and to march to Red Heath, south of Newbury, on 22 October. Donnington Castle siege had been raised by the parliamentarians themselves, and so the King sent cavalry under the earl of Northampton to attempt the relief of Banbury garrison. This move reduced the King's army in strength by about a tenth, and it is apparent that he intended not to fight a battle, but to seek winter-quarters and hope to force the enemy to retire themselves.

The parliamentary commanders, however, were proving keen on provoking a battle, and on 25 October marched to Thatcham, three miles from the royalist army at Newbury and by nightfall on the 26th the armies faced each other north of the town. The royalists appeared to be in a particularly strong position, their lines drawn up around the fortified points of Newbury itself, Donnington Castle and Shaw House, and protected by the River Kennet to the rear and the Lambourn on the left flank. The problem for the parliamentary generals was how to dislodge the royalists, for a frontal assault was out of the question. The commanders — Waller, Manchester, Skippon, Balfour and Harrington — resolved to risk splitting their army, and to send forces on a wide flanking march of almost fourteen miles via Hermitage and Winterbourne to Speen, whilst the rest of the army held its position in face of the royalists. The King anticipated the move by sending cavalry towards Speen to keep watch and deter a flanking movement. This reduced the royal army to less than 9,000 men, whilst his opponents had in the region of 17,000, but to execute the outflanking march, the parliamentary commanders detached no less than two-thirds of their whole force for the purpose. Action had already begun on the 26th, with skirmishing along the front of the two armies.

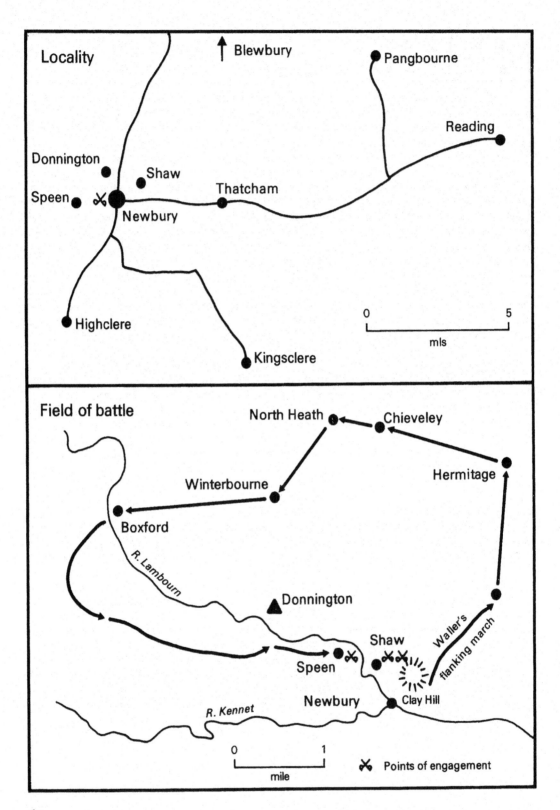

Locality

Blewbury

Pangbourne

Reading

Donnington

Shaw

Speen

Thatcham

Newbury

Highclere

Kingsclere

0   5
mls

Field of battle

North Heath

Chieveley

Winterbourne

Hermitage

Boxford

R. Lambourn

Donnington

Shaw

Waller's

flanking march

Speen

Newbury

Clay Hill

R. Kennet

0   1
mile

✗ Points of engagement

MAPS 27 & 28

The Second Battle of Newbury, 27 October 1644

The royalist infantry under Lord Astley held Shaw House and the line of the Lambourn. Prince Maurice, away towards Speen, was trying to entrench his infantry on their new position, whilst the bulk of the royalist cavalry formed the centre of the royalist position close to their guns. Donnington Castle's guns were also involved in the general dispositions. Whether or not the King knew for certain of the projected outflanking march is not clear, but that he moved Maurice towards Speen indicates some anticipatory thinking on his part, or on that of his advisers. The parliamentarian column, under Waller's personal command, reached North Heath from Chieveley on the night of 28 October, and on the morning of the 29th Boxford was taken and the Lambourn was crossed. At this point Waller's movements were seen by lookouts on Donnington Castle, but Waller drew up in formation west of Speen with cavalry under Balfour and Cromwell on his flanks.

Nevertheless, the King's attention was seriously deflected from his exposed left flank, by a diversionary attack on Shaw House ordered by the earl of Manchester which had got decidedly out of hand. The parliamentary infantry went in too hard and too long, with the result that although they achieved nothing of value, they exhausted themselves prior to the signal that was to bring about a joint assault on the royalists. The diversionary tactic worked, however, and all that Waller needed when he attacked was for Manchester's men to fall on at the same time, which they failed to do. Thus Waller, exposed to artillery fire from Donnington, had to make the best of a difficult job, and attack. Maurice's Cornishmen were driven back from their new fortifications, Speen was entered, and street fighting followed. By late afternoon, the position was taken, Maurice's men were in retreat towards Newbury, and the King was momentarily caught up in a bitter skirmish with Balfour's cavalry in which his life was at some considerable risk.

Waller's success, however, depended very much on Cromwell, his other cavalry commander, moving in with similar vigour, and this Cromwell signally failed to do, for reasons that are obscure. There were no terrain problems for him, nor was he under exceptional pressure from enemy opposed to him. Instead, Cromwell's forward cavalry were repulsed by George Goring in a headlong charge, whilst Balfour, having moved beyond Speen, was halted and sent reeling by infantry under Colonel Blague. Speen now became a parliamentarian strongpoint beset by renewed royalist attacks, and quite unsupported by cavalry.

The earl of Manchester finally went into the attack in gathering darkness. From Clay Hill, he advanced on Shaw, only to be driven off with heavy losses by a determined royalist resistance. Even so, the royalists were too heavily outnumbered to risk another fight, and with the coming of darkness, the royalist army slipped away undetected, reaching Oxford safely on the 30th. The King made his way towards Bristol to meet Rupert and Hopton, whilst the parliamentarians, who had signally failed to achieve anything, first tried to assault Donnington and then drew off themselves. From Bath, the King returned to Oxford on 1 November, where his army was reviewed, and Rupert was appointed lieutenant general of all the field forces. The royalists marched back towards Speen, challenging the enemy drawn up at Blewbury, but Manchester refused to be drawn. The King entered Marlborough on 11 November, whilst the parliamentarians abandoned their siege of Basing House, perhaps anticipating a march against them by a vigorous Oxford army. The campaigning season was at an end, and once more the royalists appeared to be in the ascendancy: the general incompetence of the parliamentarian command structure was now too glaring to be ignored.

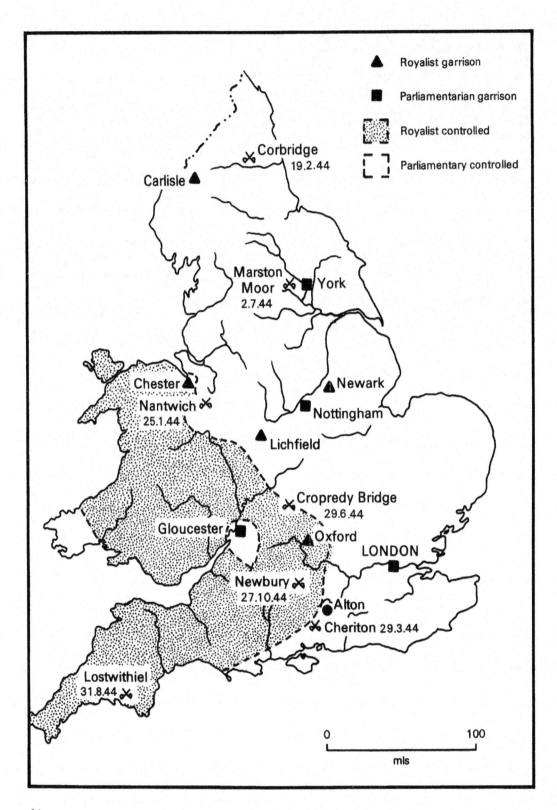

Royalist garrison

Parliamentarian garrison

Royalist controlled

Parliamentary controlled

Corbridge
19.2.44

Carlisle

Marston
Moor
2.7.44

York

Chester

Newark

Nantwich
25.1.44

Nottingham

Lichfield

Cropredy Bridge
29.6.44

Gloucester

Oxford

LONDON

Newbury
27.10.44

Alton

Cheriton 29.3.44

Lostwithiel
31.8.44

0   100

mls

MAP 29 The Military Situation in Late 1644

Undeniably, the collapse of royalist fortunes after the relative successes of 1643, may be traced to the arrival in England of a Scottish invasion army in January 1644. Despite every effort by the marquess of Newcastle to bring the enemy to battle, he had been outmanoeuvred, and after parliamentarian encroachment in Yorkshire, had been forced to retire on York and send appeals for military aid to Oxford. This resulted in the eventual despatch of Prince Rupert to relieve York in the spring, and although at first staggeringly successful, overrunning Lancashire and causing the allied armies to retire from York, it had ended in disaster at Marston Moor (2 July). This battle had destroyed the northern royalist army, handed the northern counties over to the allies, and effectively deprived the King of a major fighting force which had long kept parliamentary forces pinned down, particularly in the Eastern Association. Thereafter, apart from a few die-hard garrison commanders in the north, the royalist war effort had been confined to the West Country, Wales and the west Midlands. However, the successes in Somerset in late 1643 had been capitalised upon, and the thrust eastwards from Cornwall had brought much of the West Country under royalist military control. This had in no way made up for the loss of the North, however, nor could it offset the military advantage accruing to Parliament by the presence of the Scottish army.

Brilliant manoeuvres had still been scored by the royalists — Rupert's relief of Newark (20/21 March) for example — but these had been largely unproductive although momentarily significant. Hopton had not managed to push forward towards London from his western bases, and Waller had proved himself capable of containing the threat (Alton, 13 December 1643). The royalist war offensive had virtually stood still for the winter of 1643/4, regiments resting, new ones being recruited and trained. The battle of Cheriton (29 March) had obliged Hopton and Lord Forth to fall back after initial success, and then to merge with the Oxford army. The advance on London from the South-West had failed, thanks to Waller's resistance. Strategic blunder, plus the division of the forces of Waller and the earl of Essex, however, had played into royalist hands. The King had shown himself adept at march and counter-march, playing out time, and on 6 June the two parliamentary commanders had split their forces after dispute. Waller had pursued the King, and after much manoeuvre, had been broken at Cropredy Bridge (29 June). The earl of Essex, heading into the West Country to tackle Prince Maurice and the royalist forces there, had found himself hemmed in at Lostwithiel in August where he had suffered a humiliating defeat. The King had been largely responsible for the successful outcome of these campaigns in 1644, but as has been urged, they were in vain: he had lost the North and he had not yet dealt with the additional threat posed by the Scots. In terms of weight of numbers, war materials and finance, the allied forces would inevitably be able to hold out longer than the King, and even if they could not win a major victory (as they were to do in 1645 at Naseby) the mere ability to contain and to confine royalist operations would in the long run prove beneficial. This must have been apparent to the King's advisers if it was not to the King himself (Charles as King surely could not publicly appear to contemplate failure?): it certainly began to dawn upon Rupert. However, the campaign and second battle of Newbury (27 October) served to boost royalist confidence temporarily, and the year 1644, if the Council of War at Oxford did not dwell too long upon the situation in northern England, appeared to have ended on a good note. Once again, however, advantage was dissipated over the winter months, and early in 1645 the plans for the New Model Army were already being finalised. Parliament clearly perceived it had to win, and win convincingly.

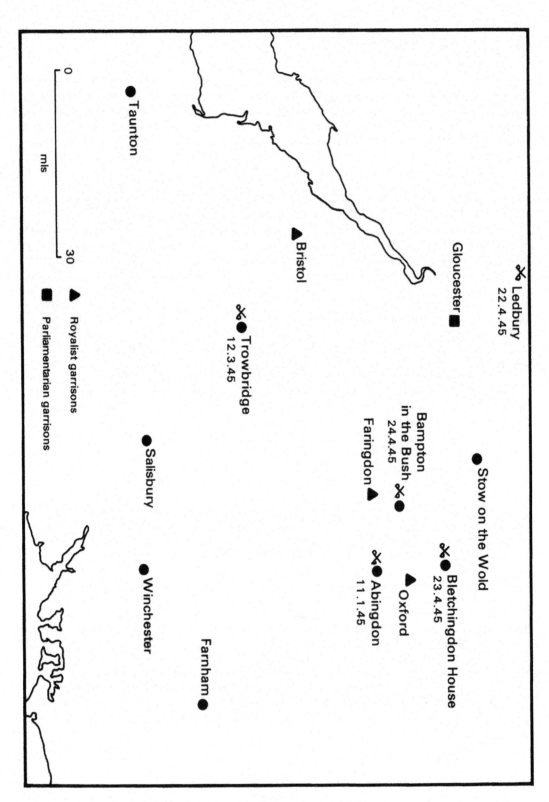

Ledbury
22.4.45

Gloucester ■

Taunton ●

0

mls

30

Bristol ▲

Trowbridge ● ✂
12.3.45

Bampton
in the Bush ✂
24.4.45

Faringdon ▲

Stow on the Wold ●

Salisbury ●

Bletchingdon House ● ✂
23.4.45

Oxford ▲

Abingdon ● ✂
11.1.45

Winchester ●

Farnham ●

▲ Royalist garrisons

■ Parliamentarian garrisons

66

MAP 30 Developments in Early 1645

The arrival of the Scots in the war, although it had materially contributed to the loss of the northern royalist army, had achieved little else. The resilience of the King and his commanders was marked, and the Parliament's armies, technically led from London by politicians, had proved incapable even with every advantage in numbers, of settling the Oxford army. The second battle of Newbury emphasised this failure, and led to heart-searching in London, aggravated by bitterness between the earl of Manchester and Oliver Cromwell over the whole purpose of the war effort. Manchester's reluctance to defeat the King was self-evident, and on 9 December 1644 Cromwell demanded action to save the cause for which he fought. The Self-Denying Ordinance required members of the Commons and Lords to resign their commands in the army, thus effectively ridding the proposed New Model of men like Manchester, Essex and Waller. It did not, however, preclude their reappointment, but only Cromwell continued to enjoy military command under Sir Thomas Fairfax, the general appointed to command the New Model. During this period of parliamentary reorganisation, however, the royalists did nothing to capitalise upon it.

On 11 January 1645 Rupert was driven off from Abingdon with losses, whilst a feigned advance towards London executed by George Goring, which reached Farnham, merely drew into the field Sir William Waller and 6,000 to contain him. Waller routed a royalist force at Trowbridge on 12 March, and Taunton was relieved by a column under General Holbourne. Waller appears to have planned a march on Bristol and the capitulation of the port, but he was over-anticipating, and drew back on Salisbury, constantly harried by Goring but with no great risk of a battle. On 4 March the Prince of Wales was sent to Bristol to establish a court there and to try to put a little fire into the feuding royalist commanders in the West Country. Instead, the Prince's court became merely a centre for intrigues against Prince Rupert, and the Prince of Wales' military superiority over Rupert gave the recalcitrant royalist commanders cover for their dilatoriness. Rupert defeated a Gloucester city force at Ledbury on 22 April, but as the months passed the King grew less sanguine as to the outcome of the new campaigning season. He was now apparently committed to bringing in Irish forces, and Rupert believed that a decisive thrust northwards into Cheshire would enable the King to form an army with the marquess of Montrose, operating in Scotland with Irish and Scottish troops, and very successfully too. So much animosity towards Rupert was there, however, that it told against any alacrity in pursuing his schemes, and by 23 April Cromwell and part of the New Model had crossed the Cherwell, routed a royalist cavalry force, and taken Bletchingdon House. Cromwell's advance was steady. He won another victory over a smaller royalist force at Bampton in the Bush, to the west of Oxford. Cromwell then summoned Faringdon Castle, but its governor, Colonel Roger Burgess, a tough professional soldier, was able to repulse Cromwell's assault with heavy losses for the New Model. Cromwell then drew off, and went to join Sir Thomas Fairfax who was advancing into the West. The royalists held a council of war at Stow on the Wold on 8 May, and resolved to split their army, sending Goring to deal with the western threat, whilst the King and the remainder marched northwards with some general idea of joining up with Montrose, a plan long advocated by Prince Rupert. From London, orders were sent to Fairfax to give pursuit to the main royalist army, and to leave a few forces behind to relieve Taunton. Oxford was itself now threatened, and Rupert hastily ordered Goring to quit the West Country and to rejoin the field army in Leicestershire. Goring chose to disobey, ostensibly coming under the Prince of Wales' authority in Bristol, and thus contributed to a major royalist disaster at Naseby.

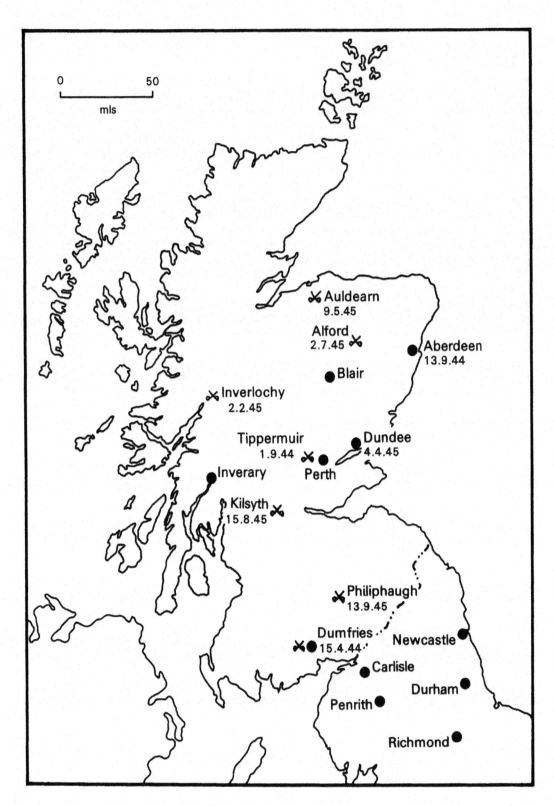

Auldearn
9.5.45

Alford
2.7.45

Aberdeen
13.9.44

Blair

Inverlochy
2.2.45

Tippermuir
1.9.44

Dundee
4.4.45

Perth

Inverary

Kilsyth
15.8.45

Philiphaugh
13.9.45

Dumfries
15.4.44

Newcastle

Carlisle

Durham

Penrith

Richmond

MAP 31 The Campaigns of the Marquess of Montrose

It is arguable that not only was Montrose the master of what might be termed guerrilla warfare, but that he was also the outstanding general serving Charles I during the civil war years. A Covenanter turned royalist, Montrose performed prodigious feats with very few forces, distracted the Scottish invasion army during 1644–5, but operated always too far from the main theatres of war to achieve anything lasting. Appointed lieutenant general of the King's armies in Scotland, the Marquess' task was to disrupt Scotland in the hope of drawing back into that country the bulk of the earl of Leven's army which had invaded England. He was also to operate with Irish forces to be landed on Scotland's west coast. Around 7 March 1644, Montrose met the marquess of Newcastle in Durham, hoping to secure some forces, but Newcastle was unwilling to part with any whilst the fighting against the Scots hung in the balance. With a few cavalry, Montrose harried the Scottish siege lines around Newcastle upon Tyne, and then marched into Cumberland. Joined by almost 1,000 local levies, he was at Carlisle on 12 April and on the 15th took Dumfries, but his English forces mutinied and returned home, and the marquess temporarily abandoned his campaign. In the wake of Marston Moor (2 July), Montrose met up with a retreating Prince Rupert at Richmond in Yorkshire, but was unable to secure any forces, and merely accompanied George Goring and 1,500 men to Carlisle. Effectively, the marquess was on his own. However, 2,000 Irish infantry despatched from Ireland by the earl of Antrim had landed in Scotland, under Alasdair MacDonald, and Montrose met up with them at Blair. On 1 September this army routed a covenanting force at Tippermuir on the way to Perth, and then advanced with speed on Aberdeen where, on 13 September, another covenanting force under Burleigh was decisively beaten. A stronger army under the marquess of Argyle was attempting to keep track of Montrose, but Argyle

was a poor general and no threat. The royalists used the hilly country for cover, emerging at Blair where they were reinforced by highland kinsmen of the Ulster MacDonalds. The winter proving mild, Montrose decided to push into the heart of Campbell country and attack Inveraray, causing the marquess of Argyle to flee, and plundering his estates.

Early in 1645, forces from Leven's invasion army returned to Scotland under William Baillie to co-operate with Argyle in bringing Montrose to battle: Baillie was based at Perth, Argyle at Inverlochy. On 2 February, after a swift and determined march over the hills, Montrose struck at Inverlochy, slew 1,500 Campbell troops and drove Argyle into flight yet again. Further troops were detached from Leven's army to deal with Montrose, and the King was encouraged by the idea of a march north to link up with his successful general. On 4 April, Montrose took Dundee, and on 9 May overthrew the turncoat royalist, Sir John Urry, in battle at Auldearn. Montrose's promise to the King, made after Inverlochy, 'I doubt not. . . I shall be able to come to your Majesty's assistance with a brave army' looked likely to be fulfilled. Nevertheless, when one covenanting army was beaten, there remained another to be dealt with, and on 2 July 1645 William Baillie was brought to battle and routed at Alford. The campaigns dragged on into August, when Baillie was again defeated in action at Kilsyth on the 15th of that month. By this time, however, the Scots army in England had sent back into Scotland the efficient David Leslie, who had ably supported Cromwell in the battle of Marston Moor, and Leslie turned the tables on Montrose at the decisive battle of Philiphaugh fought on 13 September. This marked the end of the royalist endeavours in Scotland, which for a brief time had kept the hopes of the King alive, even after the disastrous defeat at Naseby in June.

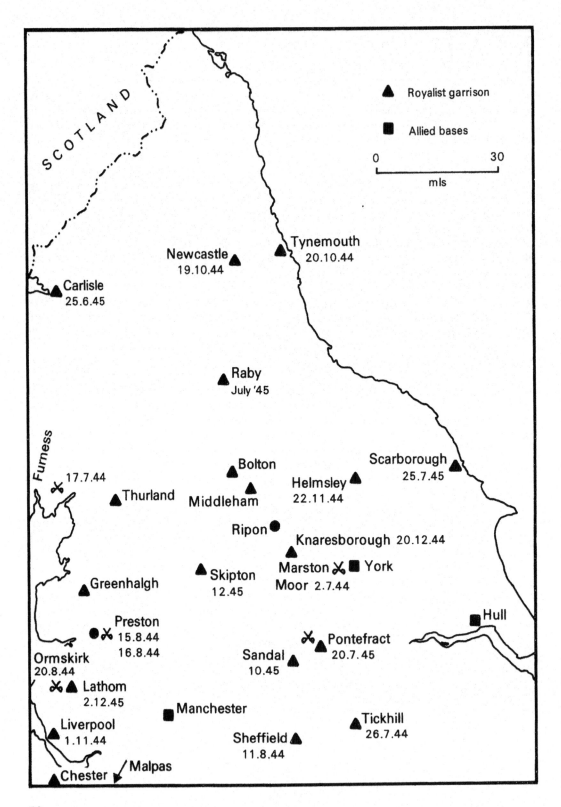

SCOTLAND

▲ Royalist garrison

■ Allied bases

0   30
            mls

Tynemouth
20.10.44

Newcastle
19.10.44

Carlisle
25.6.45

Raby
July '45

Furness
✂ 17.7.44

Scarborough
25.7.45

Bolton

Helmsley
22.11.44

Thurland
Middleham

Ripon ●

Knaresborough 20.12.44

Skipton
12.45

Marston ✂ ■ York
Moor 2.7.44

Greenhalgh

Hull ■

Preston
● ✂ 15.8.44
16.8.44

Ormskirk
20.8.44

Pontefract
✂ 20.7.45

Sandal
10.45

✂ ▲ Lathom
2.12.45

Manchester ■

Tickhill
26.7.44

Liverpool
1.11.44

Sheffield ▲
11.8.44

Chester ▲ ↙ Malpas

MAP 32 1644–1645: The War in the North

York had surrendered to the allied armies on 16 July 1644 after the battle of Marston Moor had broken Newcastle's northern royalist army. Rupert had marched away immediately into Lancashire after the battle, sending Sir John Mayney to recruit in Furness, and Goring and Langdale to Carlisle. From 9 to 20 July, the Prince perambulated around Lancashire, but on the 21st he was at Preston, on the 22nd he garrisoned Lathom House again, and on the 25th entered Chester. Mayney, in the Furness area, recruited and raised money which he sent to Carlisle, and then on 10 September the brigade returned towards Yorkshire, practically unopposed, and on the 15th drove off siege forces before Pontefract, eventually marching on south. Elsewhere in Lancashire, some of Rupert's cavalry were threatening disruption, and on 10 August Meldrum began to move out from Manchester to deal with them. On 15 August the royalist cavalry won a smart action at Ribble Bridge, near Preston, but on the following day Meldrum routed part of their force at Walton Cop, also near Preston. Detaching troops to besiege Greenhalgh Castle, Meldrum collided with the main royalist force at Ormskirk on 20 August, scattering it in confusion. The bulk, however, crossed into Cheshire, where on 25 August they were beaten by Sir William Brereton at the battle of Malpas and, much reduced in numbers, finally struggled through to join Rupert further south. Meldrum, aided by forces from Cheshire, now besieged Liverpool which fell on 1 November. Henceforth in the North-West only Lathom House and the city of Carlisle, commanded by Sir Thomas Glemham, held out solidly for the King. Carlisle was not to surrender until 25 June 1645, Lathom not until the following December.

The fall of York in July 1644 tore the heart out of the royalist hold on the North, leaving Newcastle upon Tyne and isolated garrisons to be reduced piecemeal. On 26 July, Tickhill Castle, strategically important, fell to the earl of Manchester and Sheffield was summoned on the 27th. After initial resistance it surrendered on 11 August. Pontefract, however, proved a difficult proposition, and siege lines there were frequently disrupted by raids from within the castle, as by Mayney's relief on 15 September. Skipton had not yet attracted a siege army, nor had Scarborough, but Knaresborough was blockaded. Late in September royalists from Skipton successfully raided Ripon, but Middleham Castle, recently occupied by royal troops, was reduced without loss. On 22 November, Helmsley surrendered after fierce resistance, during which Sir Thomas Fairfax had been badly wounded as he directed siege operations. On 20 December, Knaresborough yielded on terms. At Newcastle upon Tyne Glemham's successor as governor, Sir John Marley, put up a determined show of resistance, but the city eventually fell to storm on 19 October after severe fighting.

The siege of Pontefract brought about one of the most remarkable exploits of the whole war, Langdale's relief march. The Northern Horse, with permission to return to their home ground being granted by the King, left the Oxford area in late February 1645. Across England, parliamentarian commanders were puzzled and perplexed by the brigade's purpose and its speed. Leaving Banbury on 23 February, Langdale routed enemy cavalry at Daventry, and on the 25th broke a superior enemy force at Melton Mowbray. On the 26th, reinforced from Newark, the Northern Horse pushed on, and on 1 March came in sight of Pontefract. Still outnumbered, Langdale charged, scattered the enemy, and took hundreds of prisoners. Pontefract was relieved and provisioned, and the Northern Horse withdrew to Newark. The siege was eventually renewed, and Pontefract capitulated honourably on 20 July. Nearby Sandal held out until October, Bolton in Swaledale to November, and Skipton to December 1645. Scarborough, after a rigorous siege which saw the death of Sir John Meldrum as he directed operations, was surrendered by Sir Hugh Cholmeley on 25 July.

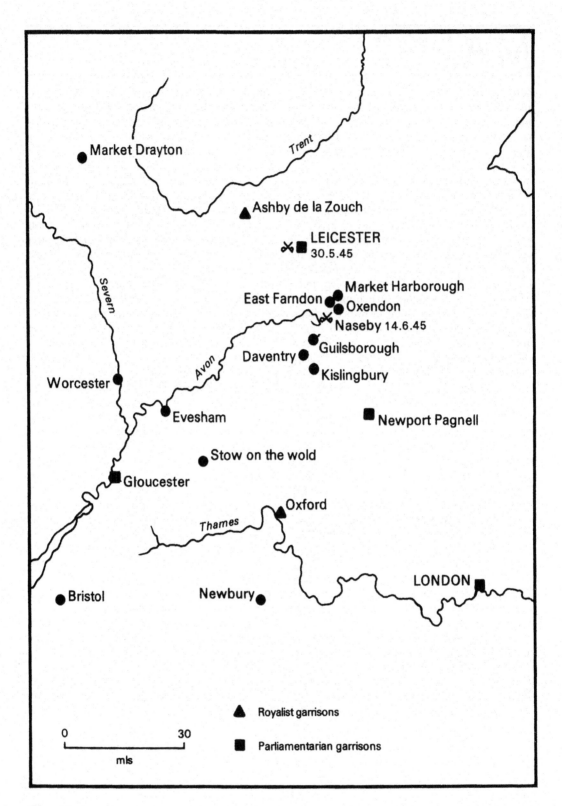

Market Drayton

Trent

Ashby de la Zouch ▲

LEICESTER ■
30.5.45

Market Harborough

East Farndon
Oxendon

Naseby 14.6.45

Severn

Avon

Guilsborough

Daventry

Kislingbury

Worcester

Evesham

Newport Pagnell ■

Stow on the wold

Gloucester ■

Oxford ▲

Thames

LONDON ■

Bristol

Newbury

0   30

mls

▲ Royalist garrisons

■ Parliamentarian garrisons

MAP 33 1645: The Naseby Campaign

At Stow on the Wold on 8 May 1645, the royalist field army had split: Goring going towards the West Country to tackle Fairfax; Rupert and the King aiming northwards. Fairfax, however, was ordered to leave the West Country and to make for Oxford, whilst Goring, ordered to rejoin the main field army, failed to do so. On 14 May Fairfax came to Newbury, and on the 19th the New Model laid formal siege to Oxford itself, held by Will Legge, a close friend of Prince Rupert and unlikely to panic. For the time being the King continued northwards, reaching Market Drayton on 22 May, his movement causing the earl of Leven in Yorkshire to try to interpose his Scots between the King's line of march and the successful Montrose in Scotland, thus disrupting parliamentarian efforts in the north. In the King's rear, however, Evesham was taken by forces out of Gloucester garrison under Edward Massey, whilst Fairfax was himself restive and considered his siege operations around Oxford largely pointless.

The royalist commanders, anxious that Oxford should not fall, and uncertain as to its resources, determined to lure Fairfax away by advancing on Leicester. Reinforced by Langdale's Northern Horse, fresh from their triumph at Pontefract, and by men under Henry Hastings from the Midlands, the royalists laid siege to Leicester on 30 May. The governor refused to surrender, although the town was untenable, and the royalists stormed it with considerable slaughter. The Parliament in London was horrified, and issued orders for Fairfax to abandon the siege of Oxford and to seek out the royalist field army, but the resolution which had inspired the Leicester march had dissipated. Prince Rupert wanted to avoid a direct relief march towards Oxford, opting for a march northwards in the expectation that this would force Fairfax to leave Oxford without coming to an unnecessary battle, but on this occasion the King thought otherwise and the royalist army re-supplied itself before moving south. On 4 June, the Northern Horse under Langdale were on the point of mutiny over the decision, and the royalist commanders began to hesitate again.

On 5 June Fairfax left Oxford and rendezvoused at Newport Pagnell with reinforcements. On the 8th, it was resolved to bring the King to battle, and on the 10th Cromwell was appointed Fairfax's lieutenant-general, replacing Vermuyden. It appears that the King anticipated the coming confrontation, to be faced despite a depleted army, but the growing gulf between Prince Rupert and the King's civilian advisers, plus the absence of Goring in the West Country, created tension in the royalist command. Whilst the royal army lay near Daventry, Fairfax marched to Kislingbury on 12 June and his approach took the royalists completely by surprise. The parliamentarian army numbered at least 13,000, whilst the King's numbered somewhere between 9,000 and 10,000, probably nearer the former, and withdrawal was decided upon. The royalists fell back towards Market Harborough, but Fairfax pursued, entering Guilsborough and Naseby townships and coming so close that by midnight on 13/14 June, a council of war was called by the King to prepare for action. Talk of further withdrawal was stilled. They would fight it out. The royalist terrain was advantageous, on a ridge between Oxendon and East Farndon cutting Fairfax off from Market Harborough. Sir Thomas Fairfax, at daybreak on the 14th, had no certainty that the royalists were still in the vicinity, and he probably expected them to withdraw. The New Model began to concentrate around Naseby. The royalists, poorly served by their scouts, had no inkling of Fairfax's movements, and Rupert himself went out to reconnoitre. His observations led the royalists to abandon their defensive position and to seek battle.

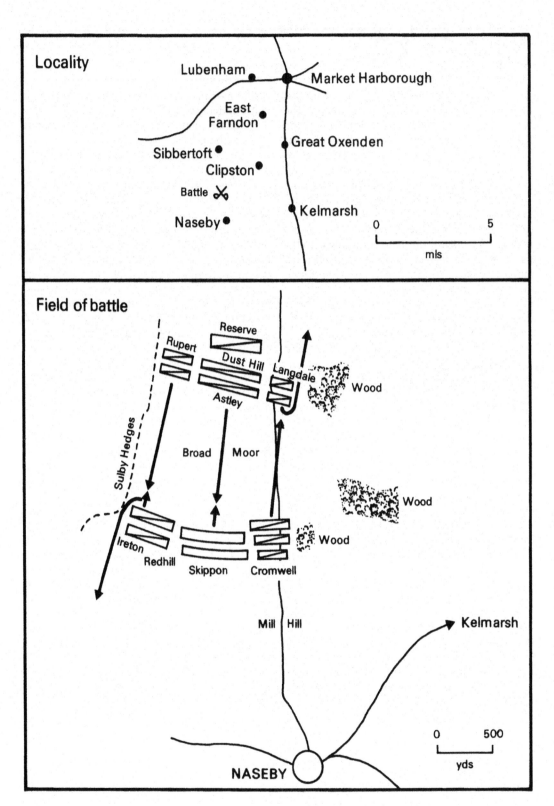

Locality

Lubenham

Market Harborough

East
Farndon

Great Oxenden

Sibbertoft

Clipston

Battle ✂

Kelmarsh

Naseby

0   5

mls

Field of battle

Reserve

Rupert

Dust Hill

Langdale

Wood

Astley

Sulby Hedges

Broad   Moor

Wood

Ireton

Redhill

Skippon

Cromwell

Wood

Mill Hill

Kelmarsh

0   500

yds

NASEBY

MAPS 34 & 35

The Battle of Naseby, 14 June 1645

The royalist dispositions on the ridge were conventional, with Langdale and his Northern Horse on the left flank, Rupert and his cavalry on the right, and Astley with the infantry in the centre. Cromwell and Fairfax considered that the royalist position gave Rupert an option not to fight if he so wished, and decided to withdraw towards Naseby and occupy high ground there. The enemy movement was seen by Rupert, who ordered the whole royalist army to set in motion, and a flanking march was begun. The King personally led his army forward, and there seems to have been a general sense of eagerness on the royalist part. This was to be the first major confrontation with the New Model. The royalists drew up in their original dispositions just above Broad Moor, facing the parliamentary forces to their south who had the advantage of a ridge, with Naseby village to their rear. It was good cavalry terrain, but the royalist horse were heavily outnumbered, and the need of Goring's regiments must have been keenly felt. Rupert decided to command the right in person, leaving the left to Langdale. The ground between Langdale and Cromwell opposed to him was less satisfactory, but Rupert's cavalry would have to endure the fire of enemy dragoons posted in hedges towards Sulby.

Rupert began the battle with a general advance, whereupon the entire parliamentary army moved forward to the edge of their high ground, and action was joined at about ten in the morning. Rupert's cavalry swept across the moor and up the slope, struck Ireton's cavalry hard, and after hand-to-hand fighting, the parliamentarians broke, being pursued by elements of the Prince's small cavalry wing, whilst Rupert tried to keep them in check. Astley's infantry, outnumbered, pushed forward hard, and the New Model foot wavered, particularly when Philip Skippon, their commander, was seen to be wounded. Ireton sought to stem the royalist infantry advance, but was beaten off, and himself captured, severely wounded. The New Model was giving ground against a numerically inferior enemy.

Meanwhile, Langdale's Northern Horse pressed forward also, but were halted by the sheer weight of Cromwell's counter-attack which forced them back down the slope of Naseby ridge. Cromwell's regiments piled on the pressure, and Langdale's men finally broke and fled. At this crucial moment, as Cromwell's cavalry were beginning to turn against the royalist infantry in the centre, the King's decision to advance with the reserve cavalry was disputed and, in fear of his possible death, those around the King forced him to withdraw and the reserve did not participate. In the centre, except for Rupert's Bluecoat regiment who fought stoutly and when all hope was past, the royalist infantry began to surrender in their hundreds. Thus, when Rupert and the royalist cavalry of the right returned to the ridge from Naseby, all that he could do was to ride across the field to assist the King, who was trying to restore some order to Langdale's men. The royalist infantry had to be abandoned to their fate, and their loss was critical for the King. Some 4,000 prisoners were taken, as well as 1,000 or so killed, and elements of the New Model celebrated their triumph (probably with feelings of relief) by the wholesale murder of women camp-followers. The King was hotly pursued, but escaped to Leicester, and so via Lichfield to Hereford, apparently with the intention of trying to raise another army. Naseby was a sweeping parliamentarian victory, largely due to Cromwell for, what he may have lacked in skill, he made up for in sheer weight of numbers against a Northern Horse that was restive and mutinous, the same cavalry Cromwell had come to grips with previously, in the outflanking attack on Marston Moor the previous year.

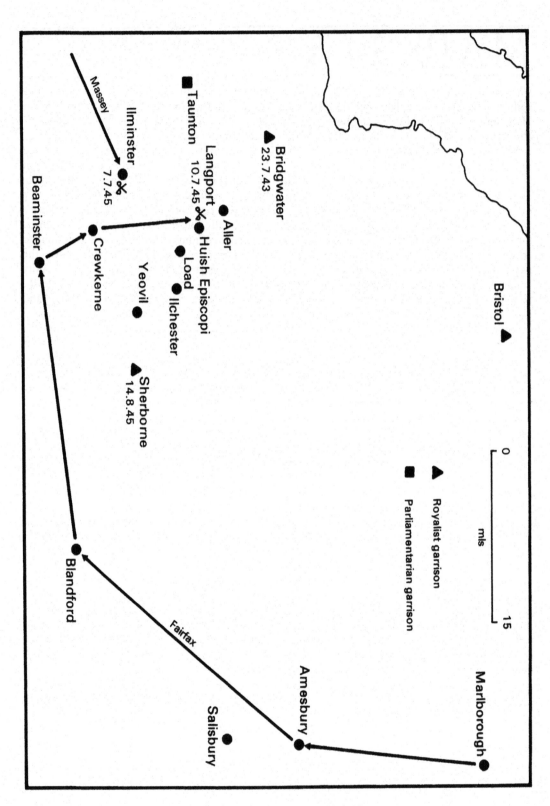

Bristol ▲

Massey

Taunton ■

Ilminster
7.7.45 ✗

Langport
10.7.45 ✗

Bridgwater
▲ 23.7.43

Aller ●

Beaminster ●

Crewkerne ●

Huish Episcopi ●

Load ●

Yeovil ●

Ilchester ●

Sherborne
▲ 14.8.45

0   mls   15

▲ Royalist garrison

■ Parliamentarian garrison

Blandford ●

Fairfax

Salisbury ●

Amesbury ●

Marlborough ●

MAP 36 1645: War in the West and the Battle of Langport

The New Model had proved its worth at Naseby, although it was a close thing, and there was only Goring's army in the West Country capable of taking the field against it. The siege of Taunton dragged on, but the King might move to the West and join with Goring to create a formidable field army again. After taking Leicester on 18 June, Fairfax marched towards Marlborough which he reached on the 28th. Moving at great speed, Fairfax reached Amesbury on the 30th, Blandford on 2 July and Beaminster on the 4th. Goring rapidly abandoned the siege of Taunton and withdrew on Yeovil. The royalists occupied the line of the river Yeo from Yeovil itself to Langport, and held the bridges at Load and Ilchester. The parliamentary army came to Crewkerne on 5 July, and on the 7th Fairfax attacked at both bridges whilst sending troops against Yeovil itself. Goring, fearful of being cut off from Bristol, and trying to maintain contact with the royalist garrison at Bridgwater, fell back on Langport whilst sending cavalry towards Taunton to try to mislead Fairfax into thinking he was on the move. These cavalry were badly commanded and allowed themselves to be caught at Ilminster by forces under Edward Massey, not part of the New Model, but from the parliamentarian Western Association army. Even so, Goring thought that he could now evacuate towards Bridgwater, the New Model strength being depleted, and on 10 July equipment was moving away from Langport to the Bridgwater fortress.

Goring was drawn up east of Langport and beyond the church at Huish Episcopi, shielded by enclosures and water courses, and in a strong enough position to cover the withdrawal to Bridgwater, which was his intention. Fairfax now had to force Goring to battle, which meant finding some way of breaching the formidable defensive position that the royalists held. The weak point in Goring's position was a ford across the Wagg Rhyne immediately in front of Goring's cavalry and his own position, and the New Model was ordered to storm that ford head on, whilst covered by artillery from nearby high ground. The royalists had only two guns, and these were pounded into submission, whereupon Rainsborough's musketeers moved forward and began slowly to push the royalist defenders off the ford across the Rhyne. Following this action, New Model cavalry under Cromwell were to assault the ford and force their way up to Goring's horse. The New Model cavalry negotiated the terrain at full pelt, collided with Goring's forward lines, and scattered them. The royalist army broke up into small parties seeking escape, Langport township was fired, and an attempted rally at Aller was brushed aside by the parliamentarians.

Goring and many of his men made good their escape into Bridgwater, and on 11 July he retired into Devonshire. His march was harried by local Clubmen — elements of the country populace, occasionally used by either side, but chiefly war-weary country people who waged defensive actions against either army. Goring's field army was now a shambles. Fairfax took Bridgwater on 23 July, Sherborne fell on 14 August, and the approaches to Bristol, the crucial port facing Ireland, were progressively cut off. Ever since Naseby, and arguably since early 1645, the Parliament's armies had been engaged in a mopping up operation anyway, and there was not much that remained to be done. Major and minor royalist garrisons were yielding wholesale, and the New Model was moving in for the kill.

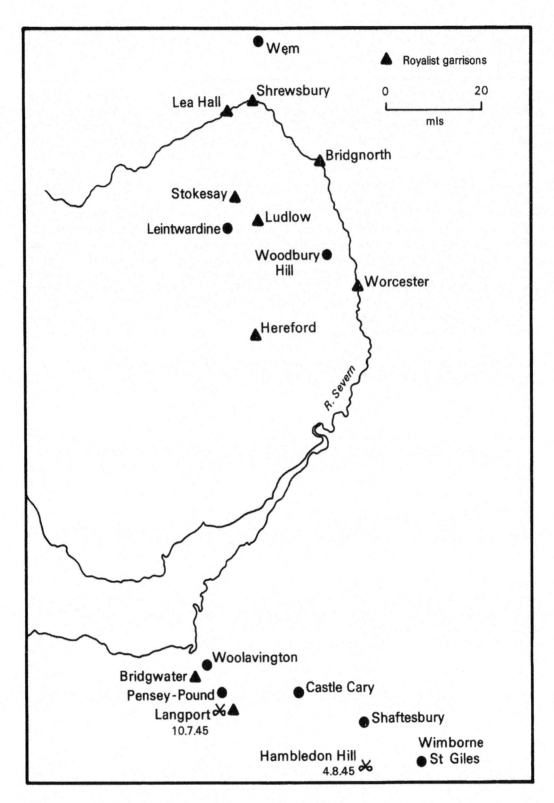

Wem

▲ Royalist garrisons

0 _____ 20
mls

Shrewsbury

Lea Hall ▲

Bridgnorth ▲

Stokesay ▲

Leintwardine ● ▲ Ludlow

Woodbury ●
Hill

Worcester ▲

Hereford ▲

R. Severn

Woolavington ●

Bridgwater ▲

Pensey-Pound ●

Langport ✂ ▲
10.7.45

Castle Cary ●

Shaftesbury ●

Hambledon Hill ✂
4.8.45

Wimborne
St Giles ●

MAP 37 1644–1645: The Risings of the Clubmen

Towards the end of 1644, in certain parts of the country, popular reaction to the war and to the depredations of both sides brought about organised resistance. The Clubmen, countrymen led by minor gentry and the 'middling sort' of people, yeomen and husbandmen, took up arms to defend themselves and their possessions against looting and undisciplined soldiers. Although the Clubmen have been seen as 'crypto-royalists', the fact was that it was largely against royalist troops that they tried to take action, and their activities were almost wholly confined to areas under royalist military control or lying within the spheres of operation of royalist garrisons. Primarily conservative and intensely localist, they were prepared to co-operate with King or Parliament but on *their* terms for a change.

The risings began in late 1644 in the counties of Shropshire, Worcestershire and Herefordshire, culminating there in the great siege of the royalist city of Hereford by about 12,000 countrymen. By the time that this series of risings had been overcome by Prince Rupert and his brother Maurice, unrest had grown to a pitch in Dorset, Wiltshire and Somerset, although in these latter counties it assumed certain partisan characteristics from the outset. The risings in the Welsh border area appear to have been aimed at the restoration of local authority and the demilitarisation of the counties. Although some have tended to equate upland, pastoral region Clubmen movements (such as those on the Welsh border) with pro-parliamentarian feelings, and lowland, arable region movements as essentially pro-royalist, it seems to have been the case that the border Clubmen were merely defensive and wishing to be out of the war, whilst the Clubmen in Dorset and Wiltshire, by contrast, were overtly pro-royalist and those in Somerset pro-parliamentarian.

On 18 December 1644, 1,200 Shropshire men gathered in Wem to organise resistance to the royalist colonel, Vangerris, and the royalist garrisons at Stokesay and Lea Hall. There were musters at Leintwardine, and in March 1645 Worcestershire witnessed a massive gathering at Woodbury Hill, where it was generally agreed to acknowledge only the authority of the county sheriff and the grand jury. Alterations in the royalist high command — Prince Rupert's arrival as commander in chief with his brother Maurice responsible for the border and Wales — led to gradual pacification. The Herefordshire Clubmen, however, the most violent of the border groupings, had to be overcome militarily and suffer the consequence in having troops quartered on them extensively as a punishment for their hostility towards Hereford garrison.

By June of 1645 the most intensive area of Clubmen activity was the Dorset/Wiltshire/East Somerset border country. An area with a history of unrest over issues such as enclosure, the depredations of Goring's royalist army finally provoked resistance, particularly on the part of the Somerset Clubmen towards Langport garrison. On 25 May there was a general gathering at Wimborne St Giles, and on 2 June 5,000 men met at Castle Cary in Somerset. A display of hostility towards Langport's royalist garrison was easily fought off, but after the New Model's victory there on 10 July, Somerset's Clubmen hunted down royalist fugitives killing at leisure. Humphrey Willis of Woolavington, former tenant of the Pyms, led the Somerset men in their *rapprochement* with the New Model at Pensy-Pound on Sedgemoor on 11 July, and they played an active part in subsequent campaigns. The Dorset Clubmen, however, showed themselves unmoved even by the New Model's capacity to pay in cash for supplies, and on 2 August Sir Thomas Fairfax moved against them: their leaders were arrested in Shaftesbury, and on 4 August Cromwell's cavalry drove them in flight from Hambledon Hill in a brief, almost bloodless encounter.

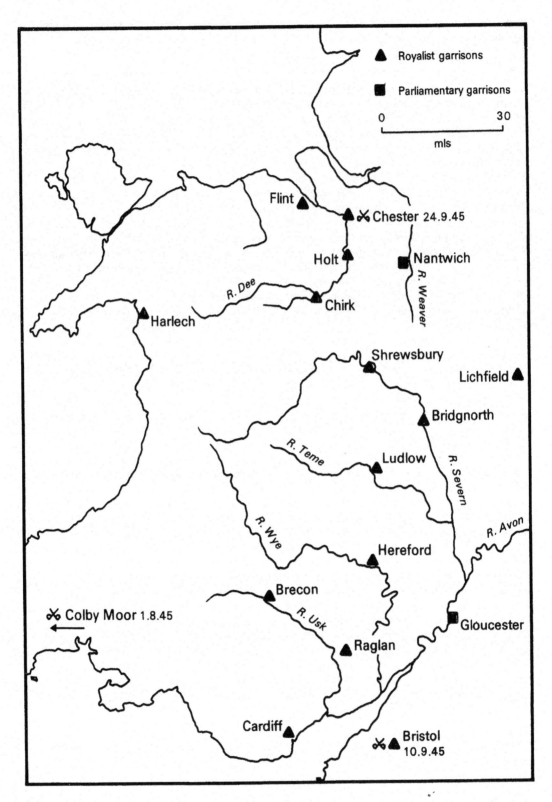

Royalist garrisons

Parliamentary garrisons

0   30

mls

Flint

Chester 24.9.45

Holt

Nantwich

R. Dee

Chirk

R. Weaver

Harlech

Shrewsbury

Lichfield

Bridgnorth

R. Teme

Ludlow

R. Severn

R. Wye

R. Avon

Hereford

Brecon

Colby Moor 1.8.45

R. Usk

Raglan

Gloucester

Cardiff

Bristol
10.9.45

MAP 38 The Fall of Bristol and the Marches of the King

Following upon his defeat at Naseby in June 1645, the King withdrew to Hereford and made contact with Charles Gerard, the able royalist commander in South Wales. Gerard had been sent into the country early in 1644 to recover the royalist control there, lost by the earl of Carbery to the efficient Rowland Laugharne. Gerard's overwhelming success, accompanied by some brutality, made South Wales a potential recruiting ground for the King, and Charles was at Raglan Castle when news of Langport reached him. Initially the King planned to use Bristol as his base for future campaigns, but the fall of Bridgwater and the loss of Goring's army rendered the plan impossible. Rupert was now convinced that the King should treat with Parliament, but he was isolated at the court, the King intent upon continuing the war. His hopes lay in Montrose, but a great distance lay between South Wales and the Scottish royalists, and only on 5 August did the King march from Cardiff, with less than 3,000 men. Four days previously the royalist hold on South Wales had been shaken by a battle at Colby Moor won by Laugharne with naval help. With the collapse of most of the northern fortresses, the Scots were active further south, and the earl of Leven was besieging Hereford. Charles bypassed him, made for Lichfield, and on 18 August entered Doncaster, only to retire towards Huntingdon when threatened by Scottish troops and parliamentary forces under Sydenham Poyntz. There had been token royalist risings in Yorkshire but these were easily contained, and the despondent royalist army wended its way back to the Welsh border country and entered Hereford on 4 September, whilst Leven withdrew to Gloucester.

Fairfax, meanwhile, had approached Bristol and summoned it. Rupert, with a garrison of 1,500 men and enormous defences to maintain, had little hope of relief. On 10 September the assault went in, and Rupert was obliged to acknowledge the situation and surrender. The King, once more at Raglan Castle, was furious, and in the immediate aftermath dismissed Colonel Legge, the governor of Oxford, in favour of the reliable Glemham, the hero of Carlisle. Once more, the royalist council of war around the King toyed with the idea of the northern march to join up with Montrose, and set off on 18 September. On the 22nd he lay at Chirk Castle, where urgent requests for assistance came to him from the garrison of Chester, the side of the city towards Wales lying uninvested. The King advanced and entered the city unopposed, whilst Langdale with 3,000 cavalry crossed the Dee at Holt intending to strike the siege army in the rear. This manoeuvre was hindered by parliamentary forces which had been trailing the King, and although Langdale drove them back on 24 September, they prevented him from falling upon the siege army. Forces from the siege lines hurried to assist their comrades, whilst Langdale, drawn up on Rowton Heath near the city, secured no help from within the city. His cavalry was broken and driven back on Chester itself, where they collided with the rest of the siege army in a bitter struggle that royalist forays from the city did not alleviate. In the wake of this disaster came news of Montrose's defeat at Philiphaugh, and the King abandoned the northern march, making instead for Newark. Chester held out until February 1646. On 13 October at Welbeck fresh plans for a northern march were mooted, and the incompetent Digby was appointed to be lieutenant general in the northern counties with the more able Langdale as his subordinate. On 16 October at Newark, after the departure of Digby and the Northern Horse, the final rift between Rupert and the King occurred. Rupert was stripped of his commissions; the governor of Newark was cashiered and replaced by John Belasyse, an opponent of Rupert. To Newark came news of the defeat of Digby and Langdale at Sherburn in Elmet in Yorkshire, on 15 October, and the collapse of the Northern Horse. The King now abandoned Newark, and made for Oxford.

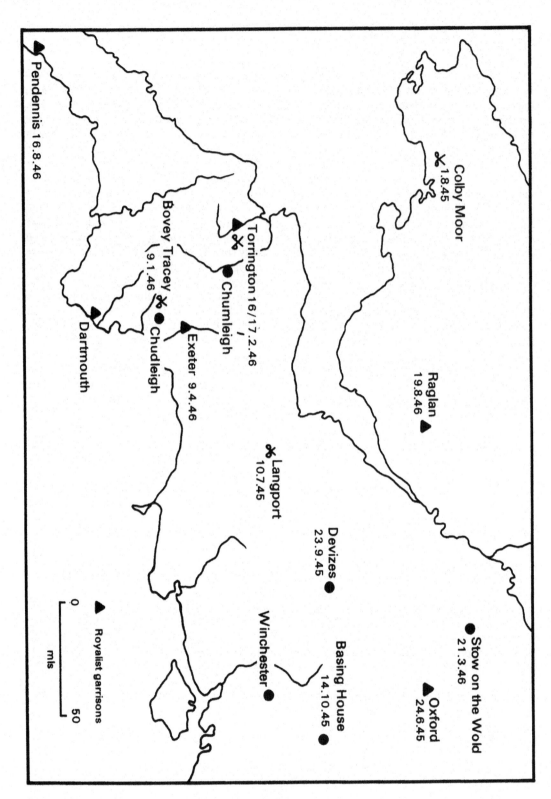

Pendennis 16.8.46

Colby Moor
1.8.45

Raglan
19.8.46

Torrington 16/17.2.46

Bovey Tracey
9.1.46

Chumleigh

Chudleigh

Exeter 9.4.46

Dartmouth

Langport
10.7.45

Devizes
23.9.45

Winchester

Basing House
14.10.45

Stow on the Wold
21.3.46

Oxford
24.6.45

▲ Royalist garrisons

0   50
mls

Whilst the King perambulated around the Midlands, the New Model Army was following up its rout of Goring at Langport in July 1645. Devizes was taken by Cromwell on 23 September, Winchester fell early in October, and on 11 October Cromwell appeared before Basing House, still defended with considerable resolution by the marquess of Winchester. Basing House refused a summons to surrender, and on the 14th the house was stormed after a vicious and prolonged artillery bombardment. The massacre that followed was partly inspired by zeal against the Catholicism of the garrison, but it was largely unnecessary. Goring, broken by Langport, had retired overseas, and his successor was Thomas Lord Wentworth, previously Goring's field marshal. On 9 January 1646 Cromwell caught Wentworth's cavalry at Bovey Tracey to the south-west of the royalist garrison of Exeter and inflicted heavy losses on it. The Prince of Wales and his advisers promptly made Lord Hopton commander of the army and put Wentworth in a subordinate role as general of the horse. Mutiny was rife, particularly amongst the Cornishmen, but somehow Hopton cobbled together 5,000 or so fighting men and took the field, entering Torrington on 10 February.

Royalist garrisons were falling piecemeal, including Dartmouth, and Sir Thomas Fairfax sat down before Exeter in late January. On 14 February, leaving a token presence before the city, he advanced to Chumleigh, and on the 16th prepared to assault Torrington from his headquarters at nearby Ring Ash. The town was barricaded and Hopton's army well dug in, but Fairfax scattered royalist dragoons stationed at Stevenstone House nearby, and during the night of 16/17 February there were occasional skirmishes. Fairfax intended to attack next day, but suspecting that Hopton would withdraw, launched a night attack and, after bitter and protracted fighting in the streets, drove the royalists out in confusion, although several hundred parliamentarian prisoners were killed or maimed

when the royalist magazine was set off. Hopton fled west hoping to recruit in Cornwall, whilst the Prince of Wales and his advisers left the mainland and took refuge on the Isles of Scilly. On 12 March Hopton surrendered himself and his army to Fairfax, Exeter fell on 9 April, and only Pendennis Castle remained unreduced.

In Oxford, the King entertained prospects of further Irish help, or intervention from Europe, but realistically ordered Lord Astley to make his way with a small army from Worcester to Oxford to strengthen the King's field force. Astley made what shift he could to evade the garrisons of Evesham and Gloucester, but when he came to Stow on the Wold on 20 March, his march was all but over. Hemmed in by overwhelming numbers, on the morning of the 21st the royalists were virtually overrun and Astley surrendered his remaining troops without demur.

From Oxford, the King's view of England and Wales was bleak. Newark, Exeter, Raglan, Harlech and other minor garrisons remained intact but vulnerable, and there were no field forces left to use. Harlech did not fall until March 1647, but its resistance was pointless. On 27 April the King slipped away from Oxford in disguise, and made his way towards Newark, to surrender himself to the Scottish army at Southwell on 5 May. Newark was yielded on the King's instructions on the 8th, and the Scottish army began to withdraw northwards. On 24 June, on excellent terms, Sir Thomas Glemham surrendered the royalist headquarters of Oxford. Pendennis, the last royalist foothold in the West, surrendered on 16 August for want of provisions, and on the 19th the fortress of Raglan yielded itself. The Parliament had won a complete military victory after four years' hard toil, aided by a good deal of luck when it was most needed — Marston Moor and Naseby being but two cases in point. The royalists had fought themselves to a standstill. The New Model was the force to be reckoned with.

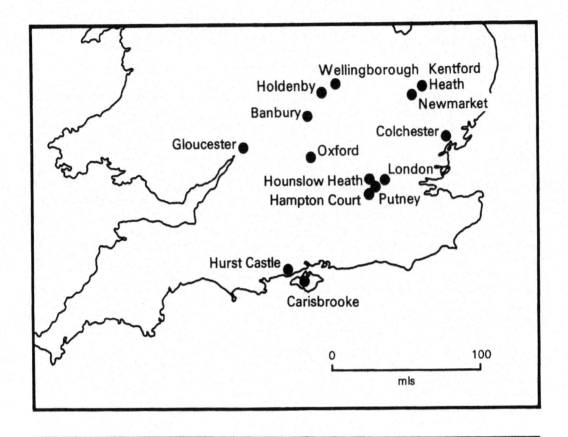

MAP 40 The King, the Scots and the Discontented Army

Evidently the King hoped, when he surrendered to the Scots on 5 May 1646, to place himself in a position to negotiate with them with a view to forming an alliance against Parliament. The Scots were disgruntled both at their treatment from their erstwhile allies, and by Parliament's failure to implement Presbyterianism in England. Nevertheless, the price of Scottish help for the King would involve his acceptance of the Solemn League and Covenant, a price Charles was unwilling to pay, and negotiations failed. The Parliament, itself torn by disagreement between Presbyterians and Independents, secured the King's person from the Scots by paying over to them substantial subsidies in return for their help during the war. The King passed into parliamentary hands on 30 January 1647 and was taken to Holdenby House in Northamptonshire. There, the King continued to try to play off one side against the other, believing that he could utilise the growing dissatisfaction of

the New Model with the politicians at Westminster, for his own advantage.

The divisions within Parliament after the end of the civil war in 1646 had resolved themselves into a political and religious clash between 'presbyterians' and 'independents'. The unrest within the New Model Army over arrears of back pay grew during March 1647 into political discontent. This unrest within the New Model, whose extensive military operations had won the war for Parliament, is often presented as the political radicalisation of the rank and file. It eventually led to the purge of Parliament and to the King's execution. However, the spread of radical ideas was facilitated by material grievances, especially over arrears of pay and fear of disbanding. Desperately in need of money, Parliament clearly hoped to disband most of the New Model without settling back pay. Taking upon themselves the mantle of defenders of liberty and justice, the New

Model's commanders tried to coerce the civilian government into abandoning Presbyterianism. After March 1647, agitators — or spokesmen — appeared in each regiment to voice complaints, and Sir Thomas Fairfax, unable to disband such a mutinous force, ordered the army to converge on Newmarket early in June.

On 4 June the King was seized at Holdenby House by a detachment of cavalry under Cornet Joyce and taken to the army camp at Kentford Heath, near Newmarket. Joyce initially acted in concert with radical elements within the army, but appears to have informed Cromwell of his plans shortly before seizing the King. Cromwell acquiesced. In so doing, he put himself in some danger of retributive action from Westminster.

Intending to channel the anger of the rank and file and to formulate a coherent policy to present to Parliament, Cromwell and Fairfax, between them, created a General Council of the Army. The Council, composed of the general officers, the regimental agitators and two officers of each regiment, was visited by commissioners from Westminster who reported back that the army was implacable. Parliament endeavoured to raise forces within the City to resist a proposed march on London, leading to severe unrest and the flight of the Speakers and radical members to the army on 26 July. Fairfax, now appearing as protector of the privileges of Parliament, marched to Hounslow Heath and entered London on 6 August without encountering any resistance. Parliament was then shown the 'heads of the Proposals' demanding biennial parliaments and religious toleration (except for Catholics). The Putney debates of the Army Council, held during October and November 1647, terminated inconclusively. Although virtually all the speakers were aware of the signal opportunity at their hands radically to improve government, the Levellers showed themselves suspicious of Cromwell and the grandees; and Cromwell, although he shared their theological position, mistrusted their social radicalism.

The Council broke up on 8 November, and on the same day the King, who had been transferred from Newmarket to Hampton Court on 24 August, escaped and reached the Isle of Wight two days later. His action meant that all further dealings between him and the army were at an end: the King had abandoned the path of negotiation. The Governor of Carisbrooke Castle on the Isle of Wight allowed the King every consideration, and negotiations with the Scots developed. On 26 December he agreed to the Engagement, whereby, abandoning his earlier reluctance, he accepted Presbyterianism in England for a three year period. The Scots promised to use their military power to restore him to authority. It was essentially a military alliance. On the 28th Charles broke off formal talks with the Parliament, which in its turn voted to have no further dealings with him.

The King's confinement now became more close, but he had hopes of some military revival of his cause, and in April 1648 the second civil war broke out in a disordered fashion in England and Wales. The civil war of 1648, in which royalists and ex-parliamentarians combined with the Scots, deepened the rift within Parliament and between Parliament and the army, and the suppression of the risings by the New Model made the army stronger than ever.

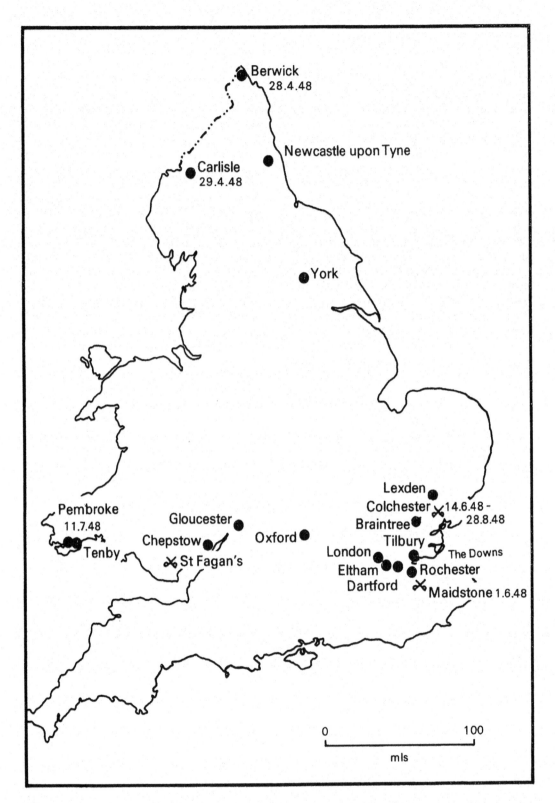

Berwick
28.4.48

Newcastle upon Tyne

Carlisle
29.4.48

York

Lexden
Colchester ✕ 14.6.48 –
Braintree   28.8.48

Pembroke
11.7.48

Gloucester

Oxford

Tilbury

Chepstow

London

The Downs

✕ St Fagan's

Eltham

Rochester

Tenby

Dartford

✕ Maidstone 1.6.48

0   100

mls

MAP 41 1648: The Second Civil War: Royalists and Ex-parliamentarians

On 23 March 1648 Pembroke Castle, throughout the first civil war a solid Parliamentarian garrison in South Wales, declared for the King. The motives of the governor (Colonel Poyer) were mixed, based upon frustration with the political events at London, despair at not receiving back pay, and resentment towards the New Model. On 28 April royalists and Scots under Sir Marmaduke Langdale occupied Berwick, Carlisle fell on the 29th, and in mid-May the county of Kent erupted, royalists and ex-parliamentarians co-operating to take several places, including Rochester and Dartford. The fleet in the Downs mutinied against its Indepenedent commanders. Sir Thomas Fairfax was in a difficult position, having only the New Model with which to cope with all theatres of war, and facing imminent Scottish invasion in support of the rebels. In his favour was the lack of co-ordination amongst the enemy — the insurrection in Wales appears to have been inordinately premature. Cromwell was sent at once into South Wales, whilst the major New Model garrisons were Newcastle upon Tyne, Oxford and Gloucester, with field forces of small size in North Wales, Yorkshire and Cheshire. The revolt in Wales soon collapsed: Rowland Laugharne, a former parliamentarian commander, was defeated at St Fagan's, Tenby and Chepstow Castles fell, and by the end of May 1648 Cromwell lay before Pembroke.

On 27 May Fairfax advanced into Kent, on the 30th came to Eltham, and then moved towards Maidstone garrisoned by the earl of Norwich, a royalist, with perhaps 11,000 variously disposed in and around it. The bulk of these, however, were ill-armed, and on 1 June Fairfax brushed aside forces at Farleigh Bridge and moved on the town. The New Model vanguard was precipitate, and brought on a general engagement immediately, causing Norwich to abandon the town and most of his army after bitter fighting. The royalists pushed on to Blackheath and took Bow Bridge into London, but the city remained firm under Philip Skippon. With barely 3,000 fighting men, the earl of Norwich crossed the Thames into Essex, to link up with local royalists who, on 4 June, had seized Colchester and its castle. Sir Charles Lucas, commanding the Essex rebels, was working side by side with Henry Farr, an ex-parliamentarian militia commander.

Detaching forces to reduce royalist garrisons in Kent, Fairfax crossed the Thames at Tilbury into Essex on 11 June, and moved in force on Colchester. Dissident elements of Farr's militia had managed to prevent the rebels from gaining control of the magazine at Braintree, but Lucas, reinforced by the earl of Norwich, had turned Colchester into a formidable obstacle. He met Fairfax's advance forces outside the town, and threw back three separate assaults from the New Model cavalry, whilst his infantry held their ground effectively. A party of New Model cavalry forced their way into the town, but were thrown back rapidly, whilst the successful royalist army withdrew inside the fortifications. Attempts at immediate storm proved costly and unavailing, and Fairfax withdrew to Lexden to plan a formal siege. The garrison clearly hoped for events elsewhere to make their resistance worth while: the Scottish invasion, which if it came would have to be contained by forces under Lambert in Yorkshire, and local risings in response to the events in Essex. Cromwell was more or less tied down in South Wales fighting the dogged Poyer, and for Fairfax it was necessary to end the Colchester business rapidly so that he could move his troops wherever they might be most useful. The breakthrough came on 11 July, however, when Cromwell took Poyer's surrender at Pembroke, and could turn his forces northwards.

87

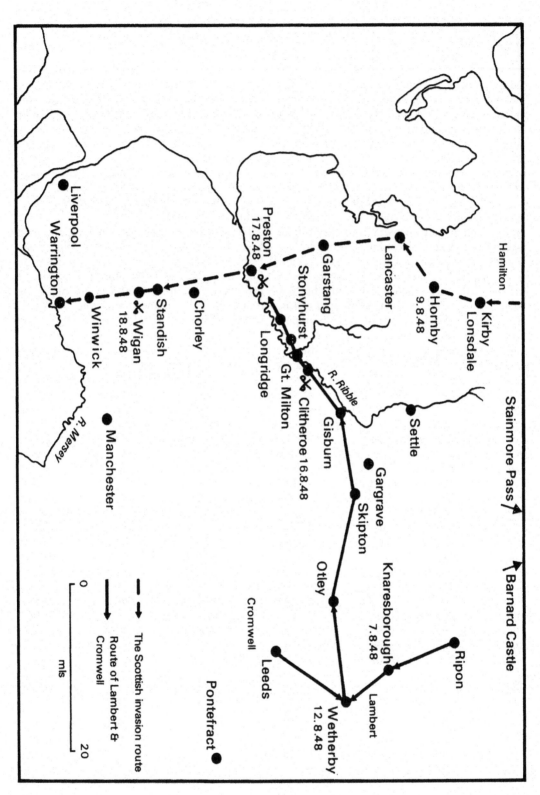

MAP 42
1648: The Second Civil War: The Royalists and the Scots

The insurrections in England and Wales had taken place without Scottish help, which was long delayed by deep divisions within Scotland over the issue of the Engagement. Colchester was under siege, and the fall of Pembroke but three days away, when the duke of Hamilton entered Cumberland on 8 July. An abortive rising at Kingston on Thames led by the earl of Holland had come to nothing, and the Scots army could hope to achieve little. It entered Carlisle and joined up with English cavaliers under Langdale, forcing Lambert and his New Model regiments to fall back on Penrith and then to Appleby after slight skirmishing. The Scottish army, about 9,000 strong, was poorly manned however, and the English royalist element provided the experienced troops. Moving slowly south, Hamilton was reinforced by a further 5,000 or so fellow countrymen, whilst Lambert consolidated around Barnard Castle to block the route into Yorkshire. On 27 July Cromwell's advance forces joined him, anxious to prevent the junction of Hamilton with royalist and ex-parliamentarian forces, who had garrisoned Pontefract castle once more on 3 June. Although the Scots pushed towards the Stainmore Pass and caused Lambert to withdraw somewhat, no decisive move into Yorkshire was attempted. Lambert retreated to Ripon and so to Knaresborough on 7 August, whilst the Scots, shaken by disputes, debated what course to adopt in a meeting at Hornby Castle, Lancashire, on 9 August. Hamilton opted to march south through Lancashire, potential royalist recruiting country, but on 12 August Cromwell met up with Lambert at Wetherby in Yorkshire and thus created an effective fighting army about 9,000 strong, although outnumbered by the Scots and cavaliers, whose combined forces must have been in the region of 19,000 men.

However, the Scottish army was ill-disciplined and unco-ordinated, and the cavalry marched too far ahead of the foot. On 16 August the horse were in and around Wigan whilst the infantry were straggling into Preston away to the north. Only Langdale's royalists, screening the flank of the march, were really a force to be reckoned with, and they were barely 3,000 strong. The royalist dispositions were unknown to Cromwell when he determined to advance on Preston and try to take the Scots army in flank as they marched. On 16 August elements of both armies clashed at Clitheroe Castle and, after some hesitation, Cromwell chose to march directly against Preston. Langdale warned Hamilton, and the duke ignored the warning. On 17 August Langdale's rearguard was engaged at Longridge, causing him to draw up in battle order and send word to Hamilton. The duke had already sent part of his army off south when the incident occurred, and chose again to ignore Langdale's warnings. The old royalist commander returned to his troops, and the fighting that ensued was bitter, the royalists only slowly giving ground under weight of numbers. Now Hamilton stopped his march, turned his army onto Preston Moor, and sent for his cavalry from Wigan. On second thoughts, Hamilton decided to send his foot across the River Ribble, and during this move, Cromwell entered Preston and stormed onto the moor, almost capturing Hamilton. The Darwen and Ribble Bridges were stormed in hard fighting, and the New Model burst through, winning a substantial victory. Darkness halted pursuit on 17 August, and the escaping Scottish infantry missed their cavalry returning to aid them on another road from Wigan. Extricating themselves, the horse moved back on Wigan, where, joining the foot, they briefly resisted and then began to retreat south. At Warrington, Hamilton made his escape, and the infantry surrendered wholesale to Cromwell's forces. Hamilton was later apprehended at Uttoxeter, tried and sentenced to death by the High Court of Justice, and Langdale was taken in Nottinghamshire. The surrender of Colchester on 28 August marked the end of the second civil war.

Pride's Purge and the King's Execution

Scottish help for the King had been substantial (14,000 men or more) but dilatory and, in the event, badly commanded. The surrender of Colchester in Essex on 27 August 1648, followed by the wanton execution of its two royalist commanders, marked the end of the abortive uprising. In Scotland the duke of Hamilton's pro-Engagement party was overthrown by the marquess of Argyle, with Cromwell's backing, and the King was thus stripped of any effective support in Scotland. Nevertheless, Parliament was eager to continue to talk to the King, perhaps as much motivated by a desire to outmanoeuvre the army as anything else, and spokesmen were sent to Newport on the Isle of Wight on 6 September. Again Charles sought to draw out time by pre-varication, and the talks dragged on into November. On the 25th of that month, the army presented a Remonstrance to Parliament urging that the King be brought to trial for his life. Parliament ignored it, whereupon detachments of the New Model were ordered to cross to the Isle of Wight and to take the King into their custody on 29 November. On the following day he was transferred to Hurst Castle on the mainland.

Linked with this step was the purge of Parliament carried out by the army on 6 December, with the connivance of Independent members. The Commons had already concluded that the seizure of the King had been an act of great 'insolency' and on the evening of the 5th had gone so far as to issue a stern rebuke to the army by voting to continue negotiations. On the morning of the 6th therefore, Colonel Pride, commanding the regiment responsible for the security of the House, together with Lord Grey of Groby, stood at the door turning away members unsympathetic to the army's case. Some were actually arrested and locked up temporarily in a nearby public house.

Later in the day Cromwell, who had now virtually supplanted his superior, Fairfax, as the prime mover in these affairs, came into London and approved the measures. Amongst those subsequently arrested was the old parliamentary general, Sir William Waller.

All further talks with the King were now abandoned, and on 23 December a Commons committee was set up to plan the King's trial. With 240 members of Parliament removed, there was now no opposition whatsoever to the army's demands. On 1 January 1649 the King's war against the Parliament was declared to have been treasonous, making a trial a necessary next step. Over 130 commissioners were appointed to preside, a necessary number from Cromwell's point of view, who had no desire to have the thing done, or appear to be done, in an underhand way. Charles himself had probably by this time accepted the inevitability of his fate and, although he put on a dignified performance at the trial, the conclusion was foregone. The King was executed on 30 January 1649.

The Council of State, which ruled the country after the abolition of monarchy, appointed Cromwell on 15 March 1649 to command an expeditionary force to be sent into Ireland to break the resistance of the royalist/nationalist armies there. The revolution in government which the army's commanders had initiated and carried through now required to be contained, since the doctrines of radical groups were gaining ground. Before the army could embark for Ireland, a series of Leveller-inspired revolts broke out near London, Banbury and in the South-West. These risings were rapidly suppressed by the army, and the ringleader of the Banbury Mutiny, Corporal Thompson, was shot dead near Wellingborough. The Leveller threat was ended.

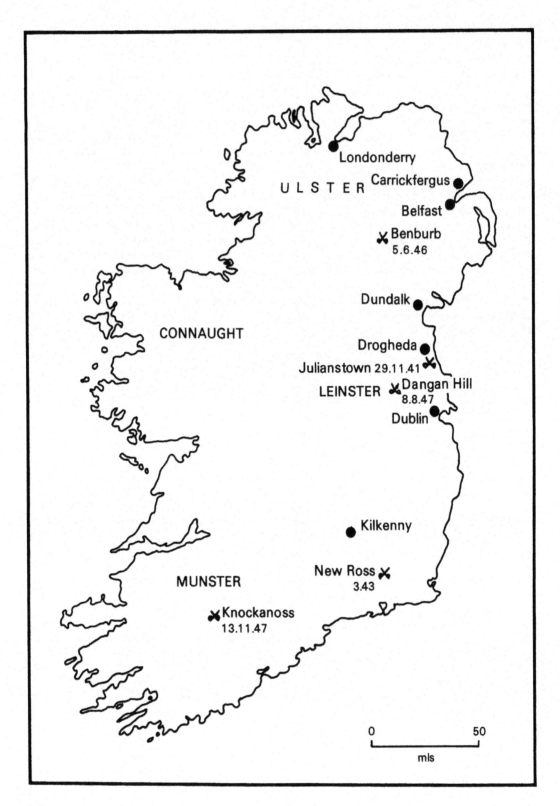

MAP 43   1641–1649: Civil War in Ireland

The appointment of Thomas Wentworth (later earl of Strafford) in 1632 as Lord Deputy in Ireland initiated a period of government, the primary objective of which was to turn Ireland into a major revenue source for the English crown, by reducing the power of the magnates, imposing a Laudian church discipline and boosting Irish industries. At the outbreak of the King's war against the Scots in 1639, Wentworth mustered an army of 9,000 men to use in Scotland, but his downfall in the same year led to the disbandment of his army by the Long Parliament. Rule from Dublin by Lords Justices Parsons and Borlase exacerbated Irish feelings, and on 23 October 1641 it was planned to seize Dublin Castle as the signal for general revolt. The Irish leaders, Rory O'More and Conor Maguire, failed in their attempt, but in Ulster and Leinster the Irish rose against the Anglo-Scottish colonists with considerable slaughter. The Long Parliament proposed the extensive sale of rebel lands to raise money to finance a war against the rebels, but the process was slow, and the government troops were on the defensive. Rory O'More won a victory at Julianstown in November 1641, effected an alliance with the Anglo-Irish landowners of the Pale (that is the area around Dublin where there had been extensive English colonisation) and widespread revolt followed. Ulster fell almost entirely into Irish hands; Connacht and Munster were in arms. In April 1642 a Scottish army landed at Carrickfergus under Munroe to suppress the rising, the Scottish planter elements rallied to him, and the collapse of monarchical government in England by August 1642 followed by civil war, meant that Ireland was left very much to itself. In consequence, Munroe's army acted on behalf of King and parliament, whilst the earl of Ormond, Charles's Lieutenant in the country, mustered a royalist army. The Roman Catholic rebels in October 1642 established the Catholic Confederacy of Kilkenny under Rory O'More, avowing principles both Catholic and royalist,

determined to restore the Catholic Church, but fearful of the results of a parliamentarian victory in the struggle against the King. The Confederacy was more or less split between outright royalists and outright Gaelic nationalists, led respectively by Thomas Preston Viscount Tara and Owen Roe O'Neill. The earl of Ormond routed Preston at New Ross in March 1643, and the real Confederate struggle was carried on by O'Neill in Ulster.

The gradual triumph of the Parliament in England led the King to entertain hopes of Irish aid quite apart from the regiments ferried over to assist him late in 1643 from Ormond's army. In August 1645 the earl of Glamorgan arrived in Ireland to treat with the Confederates for a cessation of arms and the despatch of 10,000 fighting men into England, but the talks came to nothing. On 5 June 1646 O'Neill's army won a major victory at Benburb in County Tyrone over Munroe and the Laggan Army of the north-east, killing 3,000 men. In August, in desperation, Ormond was empowered by the King to offer peace to the Confederates but O'Neill, stiffened by Rinuccini the Papal Nuncio, turned down the terms in February 1647. On 28 July, the marquess of Ormond surrendered his authority and Dublin to Michael Jones who came from the Parliament in London with 8,000 men. Thomas Preston tried to drive Jones out of the capital, but was routed at Dangan Hill with heavy losses. On 13 November the Lord Inchiquin, long loyal to the directives of the London Parliament as they were fed through Dublin, defeated the Catholic army of the Lord Taafe at Knockanoss in Munster. The 1648 uprisings in England, and the shift in allegiance of part of the Scottish leadership, led to changes in Ireland too. Inchiquin went over to the royalists, Ormond returned in September to lead a royalist army, and the stiff hand of Rinuccini was removed from O'Neill when the Italian left Ireland in February 1649. Six months later, Cromwell landed and entered Dublin.

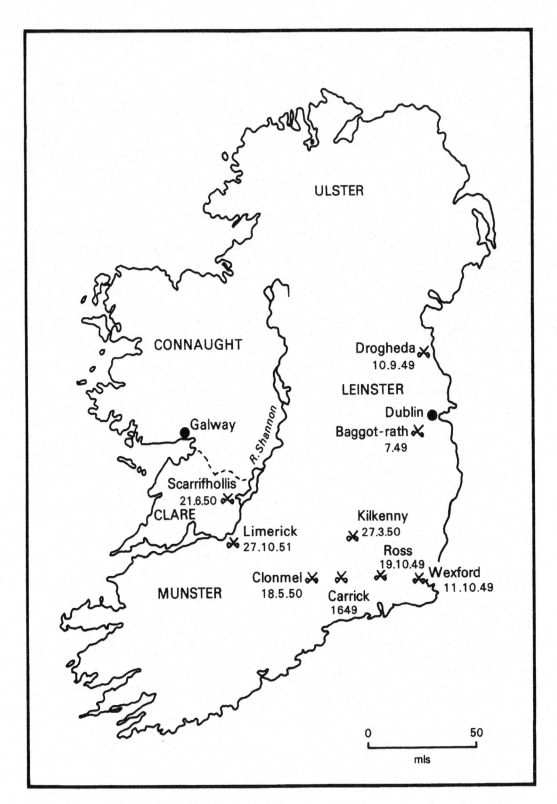

ULSTER

CONNAUGHT

Drogheda ✕
10.9.49

LEINSTER

Dublin ●

Baggot-rath ✕
7.49

Galway ●

R. Shannon

Scarrifhollis ✕
21.6.50

CLARE

Kilkenny
✕ 27.3.50

Limerick ✕
27.10.51

Ross
19.10.49 ✕

Wexford ✕
11.10.49

Clonmel ✕   ✕
18.5.50

MUNSTER   Carrick
1649

0   50

mls

MAP 44 1649–1650: Cromwell in Ireland

The marquess of Ormond's revitalised royalist army failed to take Dublin early in 1649, being defeated at the battle of Baggot-rath by Michael Jones. Cromwell, with 20,000 men, entered the capital on 15 August with the set purpose of punishing the Irish confederates and of restoring Ireland to order. He struck first at Drogheda where, after storming the defences, he allowed a general massacre to take place, leading to 3,000 or more deaths including those of royalist fugitives from England. Essentially, he was at first fighting against royalist forces, a combination of Ormond's, O'Neill's and Inchiquin's troops, but the royalists' best general, Owen Roe O'Neill, died in November 1649, and there was no general capable of standing against Cromwell and his powerful army. From Drogheda, Cromwell went on to storm and massacre at Wexford on 11 October, whilst other forces began to reduce Ulster and Munster. Cromwell's march led him to Ross, Carrick, Clonmel and Kilkenny, all of which surrendered to him after attack and considerable bloodshed. Only at Clonmel was Cromwell given a temporary repulse, by Hugh O'Neill, nephew of Owen Roe, on 9 May 1650. By this time, loyal troops from Ulster were operating in southern Ireland, and on 26 May Cromwell left for England.

His successor as Lord Lieutenant and commander of the army was his son-in-law, Henry Ireton. Ormond, Inchiquin and Thomas Preston had all fled overseas, but the royalist forces were still numerous. In June, the last Ulster army of the O'Neills was defeated at Scarrifhollis, and Owen Roe's son Henry was murdered after being taken prisoner by the English commander, Coote. Hugh O'Neill surrendered Limerick to Ireton in October 1651, Galway collapsed in 1652, and the 30,000 or so men of the royalist field armies now remained to be dealt with. The government made it easy for them to take ship into Europe to pursue their military careers at a distance, but the anti-Irish propaganda based on atrocity stories of the 1641 rising led to many thousands more being trans-ported into the colonies as slave labour. A High Court of Justice was established in Dublin which sent more than 50 to their deaths, although Owen Roe O'Neill and Rory O'More had already died, so avoiding public execution. In August 1652 the English Parliament passed the Act of Settlement as a means of dealing with the problem of the Catholic Irish for good and all. Nine Irish counties were seized to settle the arrears of pay of the government army and to satisfy the investors who had financed the war against the rebels in 1641/2. In 1653 Ireland was divided into two parts, with Connacht and Clare set aside as a reservation for the native Irish provided they did not settle within four miles of the sea coast. The landowners of Catholic or royalist sympathy were vigorously transplanted beyond the Shannon, the town corporations purged, and the Laudian church disestablished.

Cromwell ruled as Lord Protector of England and Ireland from December 1653 to his death in 1658, and was represented in Ireland firstly by Charles Fleetwood and then by Cromwell's son Henry, under both of whom the operation of the Act of Settlement was furthered. The objective seems to have been to install on Irish land a resident government army almost 20,000 strong, occupying over 10,000,000 acres; although some soldiers sold up and returned to England, the infusion of Protestant, sectarian men and their families into Ireland created a permanent balance in favour of English authority. MPs were sent from Ireland to the Parliament at Westminster from 1653 and only the death of Cromwell in September 1658 brought the process to an end. Charles II was proclaimed King in Dublin in May 1660 without resistance, the army leaders choosing to follow the example of Monck in England. Charles II acknowledged their active aid or acquiescence by allowing the old rulers to remain in power and sanctioning their positions with titles. The old Irish royalists gained virtually nothing for their loyalty or their endurance.

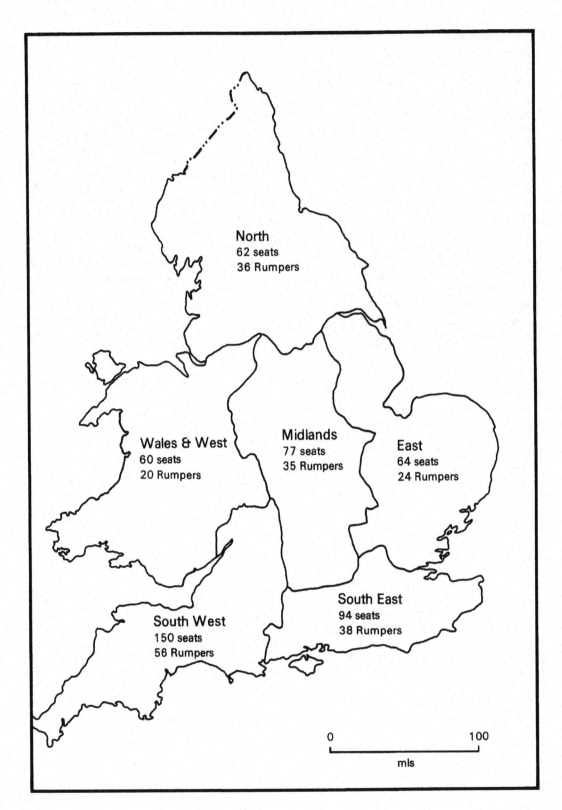

North
62 seats
36 Rumpers

Wales & West
60 seats
20 Rumpers

Midlands
77 seats
35 Rumpers

East
64 seats
24 Rumpers

South East
94 seats
38 Rumpers

South West
150 seats
56 Rumpers

0   100

mls

MAP 45 The Rump Parliament and Interregnum Government

The execution of Charles I and the abolition of the monarchy were, obviously, events of profound significance. It was an inauspicious beginning for the Republic, however, that the period of the 'Commonwealth' — 1649 to 1653 — was marked by the government of the Rump, a minority element of the Long Parliament. This proved to be strikingly unpopular (although its corruption was exaggerated), and not overly dedicated to the current revolutionary sentiments. And from its very inception, the morale of the Republican regime was low. The Rump ruled as the Long Parliament had done, by committee, whether of the house or of the localities. The elective Council of State, successor to the Committee of Both Kingdoms, acted as the executive, and was largely civilian in make-up. The successful campaigns in Ireland and Scotland conducted under the aegis of the Commonwealth, were in fact the victories of the army and, in particular, of Cromwell, who generally sympathised with the religious policies of the Rump — mild Presbyterianism within the State Church and the flourishing of sects. In foreign policy, the Rump was aligned very closely with the commercial interests of the City of London, occasioning the Navigation Act of 1651 and the prosecution of a costly war with a potential ally, the United Provinces of the Netherlands, arising from colonial rivalry. The army viewed the civilian regime with increasing suspicion, fed partly by the Rump's unwillingness to arrive at a constitutional settlement, and partly by the propaganda of Levellers, disenchanted religious radicals and royalists. Increasing confrontation between the Rump and radical religious elements in the army headed by Major General Thomas Harrison contributed to the Rump's downfall in 1653, dissolved by Cromwell whose authority lay in the mailed fist of the force he commanded. Succeeded briefly by the Nominated Parliament, the Rump was eventually replaced in December 1653 by the Protectorate. The Nominated Parliament, mouthpiece of radical puritans in the army and known popularly as Barebone's Parliament, was an experiment that failed, but one that was apparently dear to Cromwell himself. The Protectorate itself rose upon a written constitution, the Instrument of Government, framed by John Lambert, and intended to restrict the potential for Cromwell's personal authority to develop into despotism. Cromwell may have enjoyed a marginally wider power base than had the Rump, despite being opposed by most ex-Rumpers as well as the Republic's conventional enemies.

The radical puritan element in the army needed to be suppressed, and 'purges' extended to members of the Parliaments of 1654 and 1656. The rule of the Major Generals, instituted in 1655, was a response to royalist activism but also an acknowledgement of the difficulty of reconciliation which Cromwell clearly desired. The Major Generals disappeared once Parliament pronounced against them and after 1656 there was a move towards a more civilian regime, coupled with Cromwell's rejection of the offer of a crown made by Parliament. Cromwell's reasons for refusing the crown have always been unclear but were probably partly due to his fear of the consequences, and partly due also to his concept of how the country ought in future to be governed. In 1657, however, the acceptance of the Humble Petition and Advice turned the restrictive Council of State into a subordinate body reliant upon the person of the Protector for its authority. At Cromwell's death in 1658 the government was in serious debt as a result of heavy military expenditure, the country was involved in an increasingly unpopular war with Spain, and the army had had to be purged of restive elements. On the credit side, the national standing was high abroad, in that European countries entertained a healthy respect for the young Republic, but internally the country was unstable, not only because of rival elements within it, but chiefly because there had been no satisfactory constitutional settlement following upon the abolition of monarchy. The fall of Richard Cromwell and the return of the Rump signified this. Reconciliation of conflicting views and loyalties had proved impossible to achieve.

Orkney Islands

Thurso

Dunbeath

Kyle
Dunrobin
Carbisdale 27.4.50

Inverness

Brechin

Edinburgh
Berwick

Newcastle

Gloucester
Oxford
Wallingford
Bristol
London

Weymouth
Portland

Isles of Scilly

Jersey

0   100
mls

MAP 46 1650–1651: The Outbreak of the Third Civil War

The failure of the 1648 rising was largely due to the inability of the Scots either to act in unison or to act positively. In the attitude to Charles II in Scotland, there was more or less a three-way split: the old Montrose royalists, the Engagers (residue of Hamilton's party) and the hard-line Covenanters. The two latter shared a mutual dislike of Montrose. It was unfortunate for Charles II, therefore, that after the events of 1649/50 he was obliged to depend upon the Scots for a military resolution of his pretensions. Initially he looked to risings within England, and to a resurgent Montrose, to achieve his ends, but he looked in vain. On 23 March 1650 Montrose landed on the Orkneys, crossed the Pentland Firth into Sutherland on 12 April and began to raise forces. He took Thurso and Dunbeath Castle, but was repulsed from before Dunrobin and turned back into the Kyle of Sutherland. A force from David Leslie's covenanting army established at Brechin, moved from its base at Inverness and slaughtered the royalist forces near Carbisdale. Montrose was taken, tried, and hanged in Edinburgh on 21 May.

Charles II did not move rapidly into *rapprochement* with the Covenanters. Although the Queen Mother and her favourite, Henry Jermyn, through the Louvre Group (Catholics who favoured a scottish alliance), dominated policy decisions at the court in exile, Charles still hoped for something from the old cavaliers in England. They, however, lacked the resources, the manpower and the major landowners to foment anything but patchy unrest, however well-intentioned. With royalist garrisons still intact in the Isles of Scilly and on Jersey, the likeliest area for action would be the South-West of England, and particularly Cornwall, which had proved itself doggedly loyal during the first civil war. The royalists moved easily about the sea lanes, and in July 1650 there were abortive minor risings in Portland and Weymouth. A Western Association was formed to co-ordinate plans, secret gatherings of cavaliers under the cover

of race meetings were frequent, and the government embarked on a series of arrests to nip plots in the bud. The regicide, Thomas Scot, directed effective intelligence operations for the Council of State, the machinery later taken over and made more effective by John Thurloe. Throughout England, royalist groups came together and dispersed without achieving anything, and only the Western Association seems to have developed a network of reliable supporters, extending into Gloucestershire and the Welsh border country. Laudable as it was, it was not enough, and on 23 June 1650 Charles II arrived in Scotland and took the Covenant with much distaste and considerable personal reservations, as a means of gaining for himself the armed support of Scotland. The Covenanters, having dealt with Montrose, and having barred the Engagers from involvement, were now more than willing to assist the King, and David Leslie began to raise a formidable army. The English government, however, were kept well-informed, and began to expect some Scottish action or other long before June; the Council of State was resolved to strike first. Cromwell, returning from his triumphant campaigns in Ireland, was an advocate of this policy, but Sir Thomas Fairfax, commander of the New Model, resisted it — he seems to have begun to mislike his position since the execution of Charles I. Parliament voted for an invasion of Scotland on 20 June, Fairfax argued that this breached their earlier agreement with that kingdom made in 1643, and on 26 June resigned his commission. His place was filled by Cromwell, troops were posted at the crucial towns of London, Oxford, Newcastle, Bristol, Gloucester, Wallingford and Berwick to contain the country in the event of a rising, and old elements of the provincial armies were called out again. A marching army of 15,000 men was prepared, and on 19 July this force was at Berwick. It crossed into Scotland on 22 July.

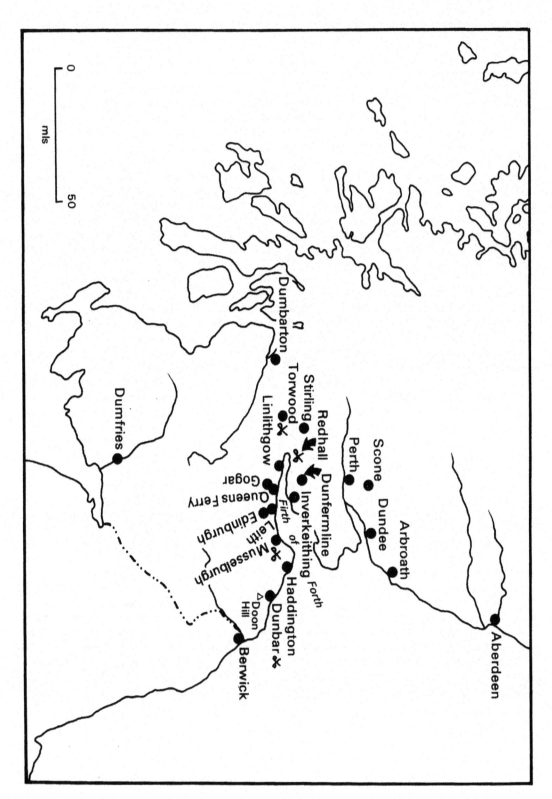

MAP 47 1650: The Dunbar Campaign

David Leslie's Scottish army, although superior in numbers, was in fact not up to scratch, the direct consequence of the hard line taken by the Covenanters. Ex-royalists were barred from serving, whether Scottish or English, thus depriving the army of good commanders and large numbers of veteran troops. The regiments were largely raw and inexperienced, whilst those of the New Model were battle-hardened. Cromwell's *de facto* second in command was John Lambert, his major general of the cavalry.

When Cromwell crossed into Scotland on 22 July, David Leslie's army was drawn up defensively between Edinburgh and Leith, the country was stripped of provisions, and the English were thus obliged to move along the sea coast to obtain war materials from the navy. Between Berwick and Edinburgh lay the port of Dunbar. Cromwell occupied the port on 26 July, then moved on to Haddington, Lambert skirmishing with Scottish forces near Musselburgh, around which point the English army quartered. Lambert's attempt to fall back on the main body at that place induced Leslie to launch an attack on him, but after hard fighting in which Lambert was wounded and almost fell into enemy hands, the English cavalry drove off their Scottish counterparts. On 31 July Scottish cavalry under Robert Montgomery launched an attack on the dispirited English at Musselburgh, but despite initial success, failed to achieve anything, and withdrew. The Musselburgh position was untenable for, due to stormy and wet weather, it had proved impossible to land supplies at Dunbar for conveying to the encamped army, and about a third of the English army had been rendered useless due to casualties in the fighting or to ailments associated with the wretched weather. Cromwell, therefore, drew off towards Dunbar, returning to Musselburgh on 12 August. Acting a

little more energetically, he had decided to try to turn the Scottish flank and march in co-ordination with the movement of his ships down the Firth of Forth. This imaginative plan came to nothing, and after assaulting and taking a Scottish strongpoint at Redhall on 26 August, Cromwell moved to the west towards Stirling.

The Scottish army marched parallel to him, drawing up on excellent defensive ground near Gogar. The English, unable to launch an assault, again withdrew to Musselburgh, whilst David Leslie withdrew towards Edinburgh. The New Model had been out-marched and out-manoeuvred, and Cromwell knew it. On 31 August he ordered a general withdrawal to Dunbar, followed at a distance by Scottish cavalry. The English took up positions around Dunbar anticipating an attack, for the fall of Dunbar would wreck the army by depriving it of essential supplies: morale was anyway very low. On 1 September David Leslie tightened the net around the port by closing its only road link, forcing the English either to fight with nowhere to run to, or else to evacuate. Leslie, who had come through Marston Moor in July 1644 much in Cromwell's shadow, had shown himself the better general. He now swung to the south of Dunbar, occupied Doon Hill, and so stood between the English and Berwick. On 2 September the Scottish forces prepared for battle, and it seems that Leslie intended an all-out assault on the port. It may be that he believed Cromwell was already organising an evacuation, in which case he was wrong. Whilst his army was well positioned for an attack, it was no longer secure defensively, and this Cromwell was able to see from Dunbar. Having advocated a pre-emptive strike into Scotland, Cromwell now determined to break out of Dunbar with a single battle, taking the war to the enemy.

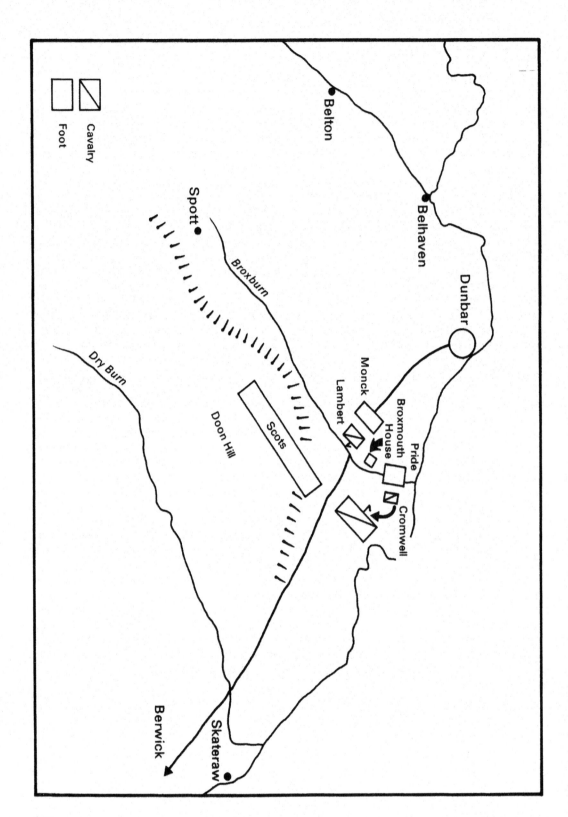

Cavalry

Foot

Belton

Spott

Broxburn

Dry Burn

Doon Hill

Scots

Belhaven

Dunbar

Monck

Lambert

Broxmouth House

Pride

Cromwell

Berwick

Skateraw

MAP 48 The Battle of Dunbar, 3 September 1650 and Its Aftermath

On 2 September preparatory to an assault on Dunbar, Leslie had put the bulk of his cavalry on the right flank between the road to Berwick and the coast, whilst his infantry lay between the road and their original position on Doon Hill. His army was perhaps 22,000 strong, more than double the size of the New Model, and Cromwell's decision to attack was by no means popular with his commanders. However, he carried the day at a hastily summoned council of war, where it was decided that a straightforward frontal assault along the Berwick road would be attempted. The foul weather showed no sign of abating, and it may be that the Scots were lulled into believing such an attack was improbable. Thus, when just before daybreak on 3 September Lambert crossed the Broxburn and reformed for his attack, he met light resistance and stormed into the enemy cavalry lines with the maximum of impact. After giving ground, the Scots rallied and by sheer weight of numbers held Lambert at bay. The Scottish infantry found themselves engaged by George Monck's cavalry. Cromwell himself now moved into the attack, passing between Broxmouth House and the coast, and this charge coupled with Lambert's renewed pressure, put the Scottish cavalry to flight. Their infantry collapsed — 10,000 were taken prisoner — and Leslie withdrew in all haste towards Stirling. It was a massive defeat, all the more so in that it was unexpected. The New Model marched on Edinburgh, occupied the town, and besieged the castle (which fell in December), whilst Cromwell made movements towards Stirling but, on 17 September, refused to attempt an assault, and withdrew to Edinburgh.

Charles II, very much out of it all at Perth, now tried to assemble an army of Covenanters and royalists. Some of the Covenanter army, who were hostile to alliance with royalists but resolved to fight Cromwell, chose to operate alone and were systematically broken by the New Model. On 1 January 1651 Charles was crowned at Scone in a humiliating ceremony, although he was more able to endure it than his father would have been. A lull in operations prevailed until June, Cromwell being incapacitated through illness, and David Leslie trying to recruit a new field army. This royalist army was more truly that, since it included not only numbers of old cavaliers from both sides of the border, but also had, as its commander of the English, the ex-parliamentarian Edward Massey. On 30 June, Cromwell, also heavily reinforced from England, marched out towards Linlithgow, with David Leslie, second in command to Charles II but *de facto* commander, established at Torwood. After skirmishing between the two armies, Cromwell decided not to try to force a battle, and withdrew upon Linlithgow on 13 July. Three days later elements of the New Model crossed the Forth near Queensferry to come between Leslie and the King in Perth, and were reinforced on 19/20 July by Lambert. A Scottish force, almost 5,000 strong, sent to counter such a move, hesitated, began to withdraw, and was promptly attacked by Lambert who killed and took almost half of the enemy. David Leslie made as if to launch a counter-attack, moved towards Inverkeithing, but withdrew instead to Stirling. Cromwell now had the momentum in his favour, ferried more men across the Forth, and crossed over himself, coming before Perth on 31 July. Charles II and Leslie disputed as to the best course to take, Leslie favouring a direct battle, but Charles resolved upon a march into England, and left Perth on 1 August, the town surrendering next day. Cromwell now had to pursue the King's army, since Charles' objective was almost certainly London, and the capital had no means of resisting him. By 6 August advance regiments of the New Model were on the Tyne, Newcastle was garrisoned, and so was Carlisle.

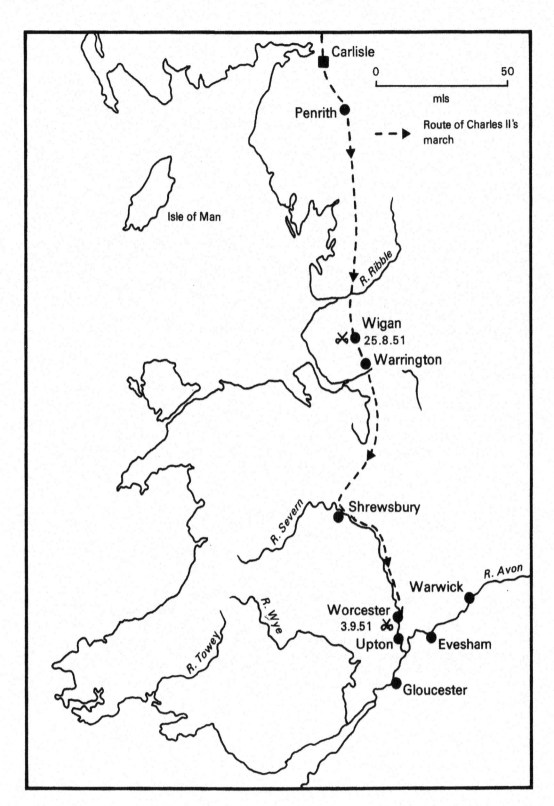

MAP 49 1651: The Worcester Campaign

Cromwell's orders to his commanders were urgent once news of the King's march south was confirmed. Leaving forces to take Stirling, Cromwell sent Lambert with 4,000 cavalry to move rapidly into England with the object of attacking the royalist army in column of march. In England itself, the New Model was being reinforced by local levies, as the need to prevent the King from reaching London grew more apparent. Charles skirted the government garrison in Carlisle and entered Penrith on 8 August, whilst Edward Massey rode on in advance to try to whip up recruits for the army. The bitterness within the royalist army, between Scots and old cavaliers, was chronic, and Massey, politically and religiously a Presbyterian, was unable to draw in recruits to a King so obviously under the thumb of the Scottish Covenanters. Lancashire was entered, and the earl of Derby forsook his fortified Isle of Man to join the King and begin recruiting, aided by Sir Thomas Tyldesley and Lord Widdrington, prominent former cavaliers. On 15 August Charles entered Wigan and moved on to Warrington, where the lack of recruits and the morale of the Scots decided him to set aside the march on London for the time being. Instead, he began to move down the Welsh borderland, potentially full of recruits, but Shrewsbury held out against him and he entered Worcester with few additions to his army on 22 August. The government garrison had fled.

Back in Lancashire, Derby and his newly formed forces were caught in a brisk action at Wigan Lane on 25 August, which saw the destruction of the royalist force and the deaths of Tyldesley and Widdrington. Derby himself escaped, wounded, to join the King in Worcester with news of his failure. He found things in a bad state. Edward Massey, whose fame in the Gloucester area was real enough, still found it impossible to add more than a mere handful of

recruits to the army, the local royalists either cowed by the government or lacking means to arm themselves. Suspicion of the Scots was significant. The government's forces, meanwhile, had come together at Warwick on 24 August, Cromwell and Lambert moving on Evesham which was entered on the 27th. On the 28th, Lambert advanced to take the bridge across the River Severn at Upton, so that the government troops would have command of both sides of the river in their move on Worcester. Although Massey had prudently ordered the demolition of the bridge, the river was still negotiable, and the Scots stationed there were surprised and then repulsed. Now reinforced by troops sent from Shipston by Charles Fleetwood, the government forces drove off Massey and his men, and secured the crossing. Artillery was now moved into position to bombard the city, which held a strong defensive position (as the royalist garrison during the first civil war had demonstrated). Although Cromwell's army must have been at least 30,000 strong by now, as opposed to the King's 12,000 or so, the problem for the government troops lay in breaking through the natural advantages that the royalists enjoyed in the terrain. Charles Fleetwood and Cromwell were to lead two attacks, the latter from the east, the former from the west if he could manage to cross the River Teme. Lambert was ordered to forage for boats up and down the Severn with which to make a bridge across the Severn near Teme's mouth to link Fleetwood and Cromwell in the ensuing attack, and a second bridge was thrown across the Teme itself. The royalist garrison did little to hinder this work, although on 31 August a sortie from the city aimed at the government artillery on the Red Hill and perhaps also at the bridge of boats, failed after it was betrayed to the government commanders by a tradesman within the city, who was hanged. Nothing further was attempted on the bridges.

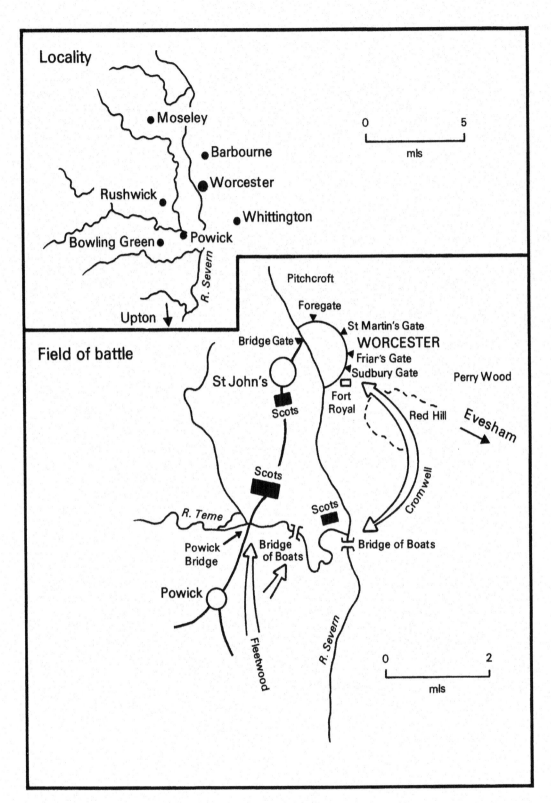

Locality

Moseley

Barbourne

Worcester

Rushwick

Whittington

Bowling Green   Powick

R. Severn

Upton

Field of battle

Pitchcroft

Foregate

St Martin's Gate

Bridge Gate

WORCESTER

St John's

Friar's Gate

Sudbury Gate

Perry Wood

Scots

Fort
Royal

Red Hill

Evesham

Scots

Cromwell

R. Teme

Scots

Powick
Bridge

Bridge
of Boats

Bridge of Boats

Powick

R. Severn

Fleetwood

0   5
mls

0   2
mls

MAPS 50 & 51
The Battle of Worcester,
3 September 1651

Cromwell's main body lay to the south-east of the city on and around the Red Hill, on the east bank of the Severn, whilst Fleetwood was moving from Upton along the road to Powick and so to Powick Bridge, scene of a royalist cavalry victory in 1642. Fleetwood's objective was to cross the River Teme and attack the Scots on its northern bank, who formed the western defences of the city. The troops under Fleetwood moved slowly, but came to the Teme at two points, near Powick Bridge itself and further to the east at the bridge of boats across the Teme near that river's confluence with the Severn. To add to Fleetwood's impact, Cromwell sent large numbers of his own cavalry across the Severn to reinforce the other column, and in late afternoon Fleetwood forced the crossing of the Teme at both points and ran into heavy resistance from the Scottish forces to its north. From the vantage point of the cathedral tower, the royalist commanders could see the fighting going on to the west, and see also the Scots progressively falling back on the city. They could also see that Cromwell had despatched the bulk of his horse to assist Fleetwood, and Charles determined to use his own cavalry in a frontal assault on Cromwell's position, under the covering fire of the artillery in Fort Royal. In a sense, this attack was forced upon the King by the failure of David Leslie, established north-west of the city, to move his forces in to assist his fellow Scots against Fleetwood, forcing Charles to try the diversionary tactic. Leaving the city by the Sudbury Gate, the royalist troops moved up the London Road towards Red Hill, whilst another column under the duke of Hamilton advanced on Perry Wood. Hamilton's men swept forward over all resistance, seized the enemy guns around Perry Wood, and gained their position, whilst the King's forces had a similar success at Red Hill. The government lines were falling back steadily, but again there was no movement in support from David Leslie, who seems to have felt his cavalry incapable of acting decisively. As a consequence,

Cromwell brought back cavalry from the west bank of the Severn and used them to shore up the staggering lines of New Model infantry and militia. Hamilton's force, bereft of support and with ammunition running low, were the first to break, falling back steadily, throwing down their arms. The duke himself was mortally wounded in the retreat, the government troops pushed on, chased the Scots back towards Fort Royal, stormed their entrenchments and took the fort. Fleetwood's men, having broken the resistance of the forces on the west of the city, now crossed the Severn, taking the royalist army in flank and rear as Cromwell pressed home the attack. The royalist army was in a state of collapse, Hamilton out of action, Massey, Derby and David Leslie all prisoners. Charles II tried desperately and without concern for his personal safety to rally some form of resistance against Cromwell, and was spotted outside the Sudbury Gate by enemy troopers. Barely escaping with his life, the King returned into the city to find the earl of Cleveland and the remnants of the cavalry in a state of confusion as Fleetwood's men infiltrated the streets in force. The gates of the city — Foregate, Sudbury, Bridge and Friars — were either in government hands or blocked up, leaving only St Martin's Gate temporarily open. With a few Scots and royalists making a determined stand on Castle Mound near the Sudbury Gate, which Cromwell found impossible to storm, the King prepared to escape, covered by Cleveland who halted the onrush of Fleetwood's troopers on two occasions.

The royalist army was shattered, 10,000 were prisoners, 3,000 or more were dead, and the rest were fugitives, the King included. Many Scots were murdered in the ensuing few days by local people as they tried to make their way north, where George Monck was reducing Stirling and Dundee. The military potential of the royalist party was permanently broken: restoration by force of arms was no longer a possibility.

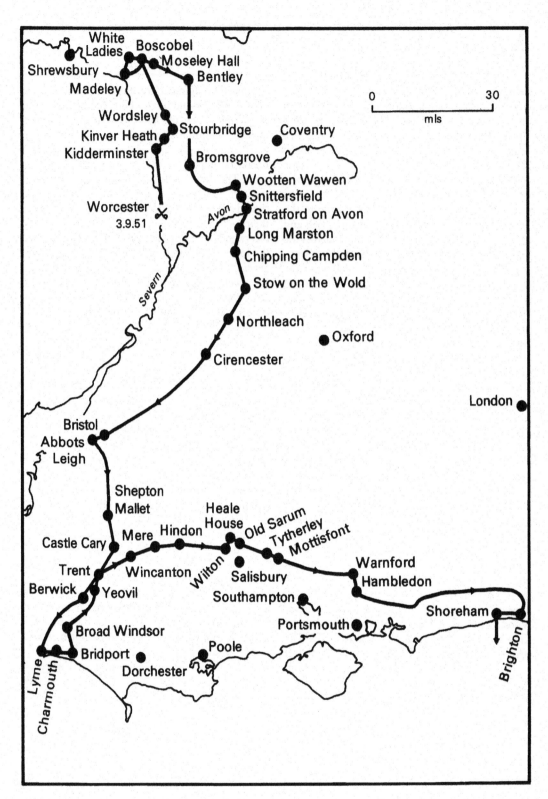

White Ladies
Boscobel
Moseley Hall
Shrewsbury
Madeley
Bentley
Wordsley
Stourbridge
Kinver Heath
Kidderminster
Coventry
Bromsgrove
Wootten Wawen
Worcester
3.9.51
Snittersfield
Stratford on Avon
Avon
Long Marston
Chipping Campden
Severn
Stow on the Wold
Northleach
Oxford
Cirencester
London
Bristol
Abbots
Leigh
Shepton
Mallet
Heale
House
Mere
Hindon
Old Sarum
Tytherley
Mottisfont
Castle Cary
Wilton
Warnford
Trent
Wincanton
Salisbury
Hambledon
Berwick
Yeovil
Southampton
Shoreham
Broad Windsor
Portsmouth
Bridport
Poole
Brighton
Lyme
Charmouth
Dorchester

0   30
mls

MAP 52 The Flight of Charles II after Worcester

The story of Charles II's return to France after the defeat at Worcester has often been told, and it is remarkable for the number of relatively humble people who cared for him during his month and a half on the run. Quitting Worcester in the general rout of 3 September, he entrusted himself to Charles Giffard at Kinver Heath and was brought to Boscobel by way of Stourbridge and Wordsley. With his hair cut and a change of clothes, on the 4th he hid in a nearby coppice and moved at night to Hobbal Grange, home of Richard Penderel. Early on the 5th he came to Madeley, home of Francis Wolfe, then returned to Boscobel where he met up with Colonel William Carlos, another Worcester fugitive. Whilst the King rested there, the Penderels worked on his behalf, seeking out Lord Wilmot who had taken refuge at Bentley near Wolverhampton, and arranging for the King to move to Moseley Hall which he did on 8 September. The next day Colonel Lane offered to escort the King to Bentley from where he would leave for the coast disguised as a servant to Lane's sister, Jane. On the 10th the journey to Bentley began, setting off towards Bristol at dawn. Skirting Birmingham to the west, via Bromsgrove, the Forest of Arden, Snitterfield and Stratford, the overnight stop was at Long Marston. On the 12th the King reached Abbots Leigh, having come through Stow on the Wold, Northleach and Cirencester and touching Bristol. On the 13th Wilmot arrived at Abbots Leigh, and one John Pope went to Bristol to seek out a suitable ship. On the 15th it was decided to go to Trent, near Sherborne, home of the royalist Colonel Frank Wyndham, and next day Charles journeyed there with Jane Lane. After spending the night at Castle Cary, he reached Trent on the 17th, and on the following day Jane Lane left for home. Frank Wyndham travelled down to Lyme Regis seeking a boat for France, and managed to agree upon a vessel for the 22nd leaving from Charmouth. A room was booked at the local inn for the night previous to departure. On the 22nd the King quit Trent and came to the Queen's Arms at Charmouth by way of Over Compton and Berwick, but to no avail, for no ship appeared.

On the 23rd, therefore, he removed to Bridport, but this time under close pursuit from a troop of militia commanded by a Captain Massey, alerted by an employee at the Queen's Arms in Charmouth. Warned of the pursuit by Wilmot, whose Midlands-shoed horse had excited the suspicions of the Charmouth smithy, the King turned north off the London road, barely eluding Massey's men who headed on towards Dorchester. The King returned to Trent and the Wyndhams, where he passed a full week in hiding. Frank Wyndham contacted another former royalist, Colonel Robert Phelips at Salisbury, who agreed to try to locate a ship in either Sussex or Hampshire. On 6 October Phelips took the King on a fifty mile journey to Heale, by way of Sandford Orcas, Wincanton, Mere, Hindon, Chilmark, Teffont and Wilton. The King remained at Heale for five full days, but on 11 October Colonel George Gunter of Racton, another former royalist officer, managed to negotiate passage overseas with Nicholas Tattersall of Brighton, who consented to ferry an unknown fugitive from Shoreham. On the 13th the King left Heale moving east of Salisbury, passing through the Test Valley and, coming by way of Mottisfont, Hursley and Twyford, met up with Gunter and Wilmot at Old Winchester Hill above the township of Warnford. They rested overnight at Hambledon. On the 14th the group crossed the River Arun at Houghton Bridge, passed along the crest of the Downs, and came to Brighton, where the King lodged at the George Inn. This time the shipmaster kept his part of the bargain, and on 16 October the King made safe landing at Fécamp. His personal survival was crucial to any hope of an eventual restoration of the monarchy; and the Restoration would not have been possible without the country gentlemen and their families and servants who had been instrumental in his escape.

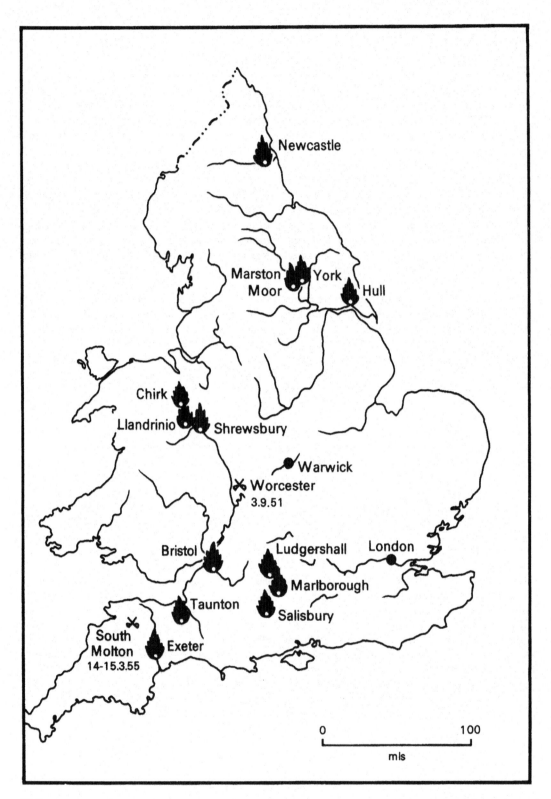

Newcastle

Marston
Moor York

Hull

Chirk

Llandrinio Shrewsbury

Warwick

Worcester
3.9.51

Bristol Ludgershall London

Marlborough

Taunton Salisbury

South
Molton Exeter
14-15.3.55

0   100

mls

MAP 53 _{Royalist Conspiracy and the Risings of 1655}

MAP 53 Royalist Conspiracy and the Risings of 1655

The battle of Worcester marked the end of royalist hopes of success through a Scottish alliance. The field army was gone, Charles II barely escaped to Europe, and the earl of Derby was executed. The Isle of Man fell to the government on 31 October 1651, Jersey and Guernsey fell in December. The Parliament began to move towards reconciliation, the Act of Oblivion of February 1652 inaugurating a policy that Cromwell personally favoured. In France, the court in exile was riddled with intrigue, the Louvre group, the Old Royalists, and the Swordsmen, bickering amongst themselves, although the Louvre group was in eclipse after Worcester. (The Louvre group were mainly Catholics and favoured a Scottish alliance; the Old Royalists were mainly Anglicans and opposed a Scottish alliance; and the Swordsmen were associates of Rupert and had no clear policy.) In 1653, as William Cunningham earl of Glencairn raised the Highlands of Scotland for Charles II, a conspiratorial council of old royalists was formed in England — the Sealed Knot. Its advocate at the court in exile was Edward Hyde, and its politics rendered it opposed to the Louvre group and the Swordsmen of Prince Rupert and Charles Gerard. Yet the first real plots, in the winter and spring of 1654, originated from the Swordsmen. The Gerard Plot, or Ship Tavern Conspiracy, had North Welsh overtones and was broken by good government espionage. In May 1654 a second Gerard Plot to kill Cromwell between Hampton Court and Whitehall was foiled when Cromwell changed his route. The assassination was postponed to 21 May but was betrayed. Two leaders were sentenced to death by the High Court of Justice. The Swordsmens' precipitate action drove the Sealed Knot into temporary withdrawal, and the Action Party appeared, extremely militant and hoping for alliance with Presbyterians and disgruntled New Model commanders. The Knot had also entertained such hopes, even of the Levellers and military commanders like Overton, governor of Hull. The Action Party was preparing a widespread rising and looking to Thomas Fairfax and others to take a part, but caution or lack of real sympathy forced the Action Party to rely solely on royalists, and thus the rising of March 1655 was entirely based upon old cavaliers and a new generation nurtured in royalist principles. The government was well informed of what was happening, broke the arms distribution network in January 1655, and arrested many leaders in February. The localised pattern of risings planned for March failed through lack of effective support. In the North-East, plots to seize York, Hull and Newcastle upon Tyne were laid, but the real royalist authority in the area, that of Marmaduke Langdale, was absent with Langdale in Europe. On 8 March conspirators gathered on Marston Moor to enter York but dispersed. The royalist plan to take Newcastle petered out with a muster at nearby Duddoe, whilst Warwick and Worcester further south and west were untroubled. On the Welsh border, royalists gathered at Llandrinio to take Shrewsbury which was weakly garrisoned, and there was a muster at Llanymynech, but determined action by Shrewsbury's governor broke the rising before it was under way, and Chirk Castle remained in government hands although its owner, Sir Thomas Myddleton, had genuinely plotted with the royalists.

Penruddock's rising in Wiltshire may have surprised the authorities. In February a royalist muster there at Salisbury had dispersed and led to a wave of arrests, but the conspirators intended to strike at Salisbury on 12 March where the judges of assize were to sit. In the early hours, royalist cavalry entered the city, led by Sir Joseph Wagstaffe and John Penruddock, armed the prisoners in the gaol, and seized the Sheriff and the judges. About 400 strong, the aim was to ride in search of recruits. A projected attack on Marlborough from Ludgershall was abandoned by conspirators under Sir Henry Moore. Pursued by forces from Bristol, Exeter and Taunton, shortly to be reinforced by Major General Disbrowe from London, Wagstaffe entered Devonshire on 14 March. At South Molton the royalists were broken by forces from Exeter after limited fighting. Wagstaffe escaped abroad, Penruddock and others were executed, and hundreds were transported to the West Indies.

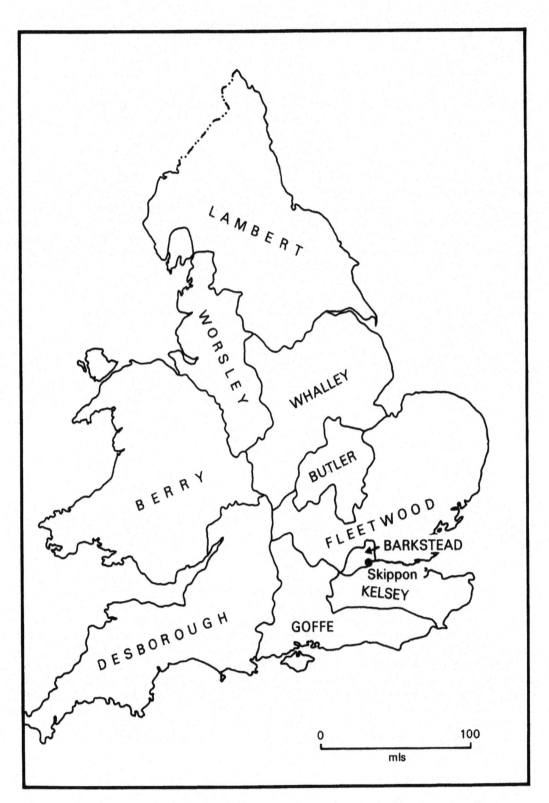

MAP 54 The Rule of the Major Generals

Cromwell's period of personal rule as Protector, which began on 16 December, merely legalised his position as the single most important leader in post-monarchical England. It may be that Cromwell sought to make his authority constitutional, as the Instrument of Government allowed for, and it may also be that his objectives fell far short of dictatorship. However, his power base was narrow, being opposed not only by royalists at home and in exile, but also by the large Presbyterian faction, disillusioned republicans, and radicals within the army command. In a sense, the rule of the Major Generals was a response to the royalist risings of 1655, but it was also the result of a need to reorganise the army which, serving in England, Scotland and Ireland, was a considerable drain on the limited financial resources of the government. The Major Generals, war-hardened professional soldiers, proved themselves efficient in carrying through Cromwell's programme, but their involvement in local government alienated the country at large, and the long-term effects of their activities were felt long after the Restoration.

In the summer of 1655 the decision was taken and implemented to reduce the costs of the armed forces — by cutting both their numbers and their pay, but the standing army was thenceforth to be assisted by a supplementary militia about 6,500 strong organised on a regional basis, similar to the situation which had prevailed in the West Country under John Disbrowe. According to the instructions issued on 22 August 1655, the Major Generals were not only to train and lead the militia troops under them, but were also to be responsible for controlling the activities of royalist suspects and other malcontents, as well as generally assisting the civil authorities, the JPs and their subordinates, in routine matters. A decimation tax was also to be levied on royalists worth £100 a year or upwards to finance the militia. Cromwell's centralisation policy proved far more effective than

that attributed to Charles I and his ministers had ever done, and the association of some Major Generals with repressive puritan morality drives and excessive vigour in organising the JPs further undermined the Protectorate's support in the country. At first there were ten regions, later eleven, divided between William Goffe, Thomas Kelsey, John Disbrowe, Charles Fleetwood, John Barkstead, Edward Whalley, Philip Skippon, William Butler, James Berry, Charles Worsley and John Lambert. Since, however, Fleetwood and Lambert were members of Cromwell's Council, they were able to appoint deputies in their regions, the North going to Charles Howard and Robert Lilburn, and Fleetwood's area divided between Hezekiah Haynes and Tobias Bridge, although Bridge was shortly replaced by William Packer, who also acted in Buckinghamshire in consort with George Fleetwood. Early in 1656 South Wales was added to the vast territory, including North Wales, administered by James Berry, and the latter was also empowered to employ deputies, Rowland Dawkins and John Nicholas. Although they might interfere in local government, and proved competent at repressing dissident political activity, the Major Generals' powers were chiefly felt in urban centres, and they had little impact on the influence of country gentry long established in their shires. The election campaign of the summer of 1656 was marked by the Major Generals' efforts to enforce their own choices on voters for the proposed Parliament, and resistance from former political associates of Cromwell who equated the generals with the court of a new, personal, ruler. The fact that the Council of State had to exclude many elected MPs indicated the Major Generals' failure. At the year's end, efforts in Parliament to have the decimation tax extended failed, and the generals came under severe criticism in January 1657. The system of which they were the instruments was abandoned in that year.

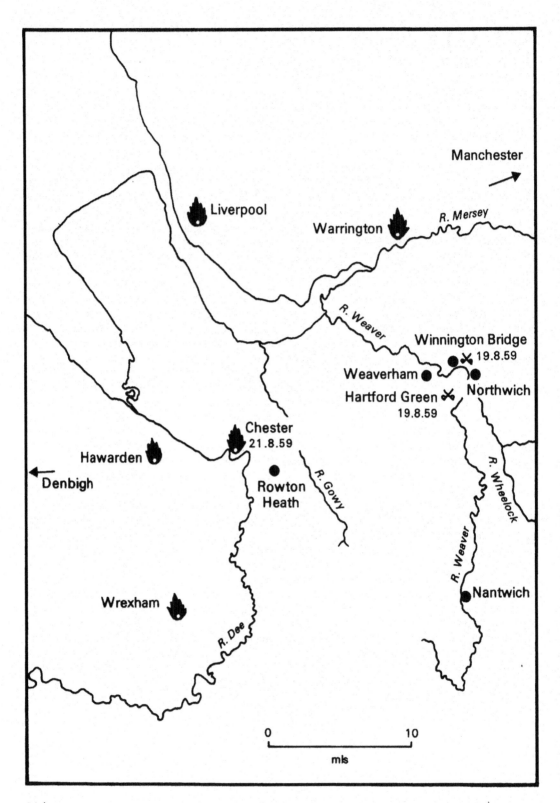

Manchester

Liverpool

Warrington

R. Mersey

R. Weaver

Winnington Bridge
19.8.59

Weaverham

Hartford Green
19.8.59

Northwich

Hawarden

Chester
21.8.59

Denbigh

Rowton
Heath

R. Gowy

R. Wheelock

R. Weaver

Wrexham

R. Dee

Nantwich

0   10

mls

MAP 55 1659: Sir George Booth's Rising

The death of Cromwell on 3 September 1658 saw the accession of his son Richard as Lord Protector, from which office he was pushed by a strange alliance of New Model commanders and former Rumpers, who restored the Rump Parliament in reduced form. From the defeat at Worcester through to Cromwell's death, royalist plots aimed at restoring Charles II to his throne had proved full of high ideals and little else: yet with the move against Richard Cromwell from within, some royalists entertained hopes of a successful rising in association with Presbyterian leaders in England. This alliance, the Great Trust, sought to create a far-reaching series of conspiracies and risings to topple a decidedly shaky government, and from March 1659 agents were hard at work. John Mordaunt, the King's most able conspirator, made the acquaintance of Sir George Booth, a parliamentarian commander in Cheshire during the first civil war, but long a bitter critic of the purge of Parliament in 1648, the execution of the King, and the Protectorate. Booth was to be one leader among many in a planned series of risings in the summer of 1659 that would, it was hoped, prove impossible for the New Model to deal with. Foreign involvement was ruled out, though France and Spain were willing to aid Charles II in a limited way. Booth in Cheshire was to be the leader of one of a number of diversionary risings, whilst the real action was planned for the West Country around Bristol, and East Anglia around Lynn. The government's intelligence service continued to function, however, and in July there were a series of arrests of prominent royalist and Presbyterian leaders. In the event, the risings were called off, but Booth, who had already raised men and created a reasonably effective association within Cheshire, received word of the cancellation only one day before the proposed rising was to take place.

Sir George Booth appeared in arms on 1 August, mustering his forces at Warrington, whilst government troops in Lancashire and Cheshire made no resistance, and Cheshire fell almost entirely into rebel hands. On 2 August Booth reached Chester, and on Rowton Heath, scene of a royalist defeat in 1645, issued his 'Declaration' before entering the city, its garrison retiring into the castle. The garrison commander, Croxton, informed of the lack of supporting action elsewhere, chose not to surrender, even though Liverpool had been taken by Gilbert Ireland, a parliamentary commander, and Wrexham had seen a major muster of rebels under Sir Thomas Myddleton. Hawarden and Denbigh fell to the rebels, their garrisons prisoners. On 7 August Booth moved to Manchester to add to his 4,000 strong army. Now, however, the Rump's troops were on the move. Some 1,500 had landed in Wales from Ireland under Jerome Zankey, Robert Lilburne was moving west from Yorkshire, and Lambert was coming from London with between 2,000 and 4,000 men. Faced with these forces, Sir George Booth became indecisive, unable to garrison Chester since the guns of its castle were commanded by Croxton's men, and could dominate the city walls. Lambert had by now reached Nantwich, and on 18 August Booth with his small army marched north-east towards Northwich, intending to put the River Weaver between himself and the government troops. Lambert occupied Weaverham, and on the 19th, Booth having recrossed the bridge at Northwich, both sides collided briefly at Hartford Green. Booth now struck north, crossed the Weaver at Winnington Bridge, occupied the bridge and the high ground beyond it, and waited. Lambert attacked, seized the bridge, fought a hard fight with Booth's men on the hill beyond, and broke them. Chester fell to Lambert on 21 August, whilst the fleeing rebels were progressively rounded up. Booth was apprehended in Buckinghamshire at the end of the month. It was a sad, unimpressive episode, but Booth had acted entirely alone, largely due to poor rebel organisation, and the outcome had been inevitable.

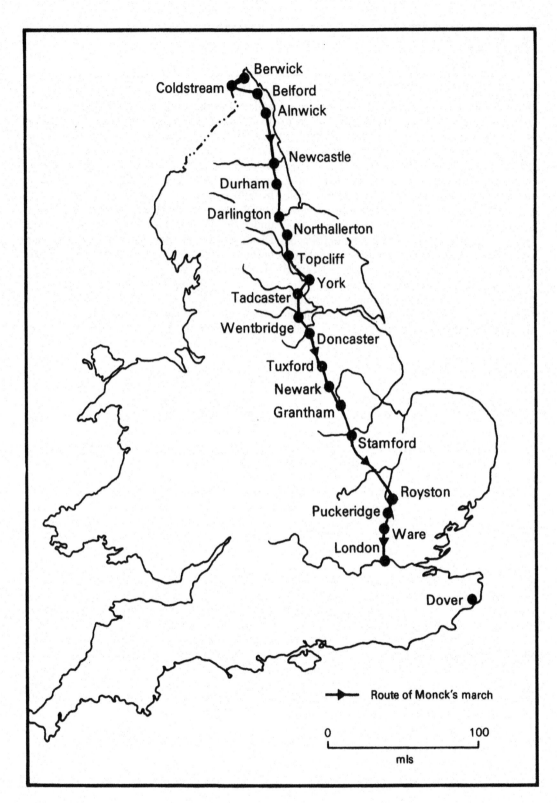

Berwick
Coldstream
Belford
Alnwick
Newcastle
Durham
Darlington
Northallerton
Topcliff
York
Tadcaster
Wentbridge
Doncaster
Tuxford
Newark
Grantham
Stamford
Royston
Puckeridge
Ware
London
Dover

→ Route of Monck's march

0   100

mls

MAP 56

1660: George Monck's March South and the Restoration of Charles II

Richard Cromwell's accession to the Protectorate at his father's death marked the end of the relative governmental stability there had been in Britain since 1653. Less able but more popular than his younger brother Henry, Richard could not control the army and became a prisoner of its civilian opponents. The third Protectorate Parliament gave way to a restored Rump, Cromwell was deposed, and the army was firmly established as arbiter of government, ostensibly headed by John Lambert who had crushed the Booth Rising. Lambert's eminence was resented by other army chiefs including George Monck, the ex-royalist who had virtually ruled Scotland in 1654/5, and Edward Montagu commanding the Baltic Fleet. Monck's capacity to maintain peace in Scotland during the 1659 uprising in England served him well, and his army background coupled with his espousal of the civilian/parliamentarian position in England made him a figure of national importance to rival Lambert. By October 1659 Monck was clearly threatening the English army leaders, Lambert and Fleetwood, but neither side was militarily ready for any confrontation and in November talks were initiated at London. The talks went against Monck in an agreement on 15 November, but he remained inactive, opting for further discussions in December at Alnwick in Northumberland, but actually preparing his army to march.

Monck's relations with the Rump in 1659 had not been altogether cordial: the MPs themselves were suspicious of him. In the summer of 1659 the Parliament had endeavoured to reorganise Monck's Scottish army and make it effectively subservient to the Rump itself, causing Monck considerable disquiet and leading to his exchange of blunt letters with the Speaker of the House. As it was, little drastic was achieved by the Rump's seven-man committee (which included Lambert and Fleetwood) before the Rump itself fell to army pressure in England, but Monck himself undertook a systematic purge of his officer corps before January 1660 to create the semblance of unity of purpose that he required for his intended march into England. He was trying to weld together a personal army quite as much as was Lambert, but he did it more efficiently since he lacked concerted internal resistance, and because he dominated Scotland so thoroughly. Moreover, Monck's army was financially stronger than Lambert's, and the guarantee of pay made it potentially more reliable in the event of confrontation. Monck himself came to Berwick on 2 December, and established his command post at Coldstream on the 8th. On 1 January 1660 the infantry crossed the Tweed into England, followed by the rest of the army on the 2nd, and on 11 January entered York. The army followed the Great North Road, passing through Doncaster, Newark, Grantham, Stamford, Royston and Ware and entered London on 3 February 1660. Monck had encountered no resistance. On 21 February he restored the members expelled in Pride's Purge of 1648, re-creating the Long Parliament for its final session that would usher in the Restoration of the monarchy. On 16 March the Parliament dissolved itself, new elections were called, and the Convention Parliament first sat on 25 April, with a truncated but restored House of Lords. John Lambert, whose army had disappeared at the advance of Monck, had escaped from confinement in the Tower, and was trying to raise forces in Northamptonshire in the same month, but his men proved untrustworthy and went over to troops loyal to Monck. Lambert was taken again and entered upon a twenty-year term of imprisonment until his death. As early as 4 April Charles II had issued from the Netherlands the Declaration of Breda containing promises as to his future intentions, and he was proclaimed King on 8 May. On the 25th he landed in style at Dover and was escorted to London, a King who had ruled in name only since 30 January 1649.

BIBLIOGRAPHY

(Place of publication London unless otherwise stated.)

Abell, H.F. *Kent and the Great Civil War* (1901)

Adair, John *Roundhead General: A Military Biography of Sir William Waller* (1969)

—— *Cheriton 1644 The Campaign and the Battle* (Kineton, 1973)

Allen, J.W. *English Political Thought 1603-44* (1938)

Andriette, Eugene A. *Devon and Exeter In The Civil War* (Newton Abbot, 1971)

Ashton, Robert *The English Civil War: Conservatism and Revolution 1603-1649* (1978)

Aylmer, G.E. *The Struggle for the Constitution* (1963)

Bayley, A.R. *The Great Civil War in Dorset 1642-1660* (Taunton, 1910)

Blackwood, B.G. *The Lancashire Gentry and the Great Rebellion 1640-1660* (Manchester, 1978)

Bossy, J. *The English Catholic Community 1570-1850* (1975)

Boynton, L. *The Elizabethan Militia 1558-1638* (1967)

Broxap, E. *The Great Civil War in Lancashire 1642-51* (Manchester, 1910)

Brunton, D. and Pennington, D.H. *Members of the Long Parliament* (1954)

Buchan, John *Montrose* (1928)

Bund, R. Willis *The Civil War in Worcestershire 1642-1646 and The Scotch Invasion of 1651* (1905)

Burne, A.H. and Young, P. *The Great Civil War. A Military History of the First Civil War 1642-6* (1959)

Carlton, C. *Charles I: The Personal Monarch* (1983)

Cliffe, J.T. *The Yorkshire Gentry from the Reformation to the Civil War* (1969)

Coate, Mary *Cornwall in the Great Civil War and Interregnum. A Social and Political Study* (Oxford, 1933)

Dodd, A.H. *Studies in Stuart Wales* (Cardiff, 1952)

Dore, R.N. *The Civil Wars in Cheshire* (Chester, 1966)

Edgar F.T.R. *Sir Ralph Hopton* (Oxford, 1968)

Everitt, Alan *Suffolk and the Great Rebellion 1640-1660*, Vol. III, Suffolk Records Society (1960)

—— *The Community of Kent and the Great Rebellion 1640-1660* (Leicester, 1966)

Firth, Sir Charles *Oliver Cromwell* (1900)

—— *Cromwell's Army* (1902)

Fletcher, Anthony *A County Community in Peace and War: Sussex 1600-1660* (1975)

—— *The Outbreak of the English Civil War* (1981)

Gardiner, S.R. *History of the Great Civil War 1642-48* (1901)

Gibb, M.A. *The Lord General. A Life of Sir Thomas Fairfax* (1938)

Godwin, G.N. *The Civil War in Hampshire 1642-45* (1904)

Hardacre, P.H. *The Royalists During the Puritan Revolution* (The Hague, 1956)

Hexter, J. H. *The Reign of King Pym* (Harvard, 1941)

Holmes, Clive *The Eastern Association in the English Civil War* (Cambridge, 1974)

Howell, Roger *Newcastle upon Tyne and the Puritan Revolution* (Oxford, 1967)

Hutton, Ronald *The Royalist War Effort 1642-1646* (1982)

Keeler, M.R. *The Long Parliament 1640-41. A Biographical Study of its Members* (Philadelphia, 1954)

Ketton-Cremer, R.W. *Norfolk in the Civil War* (1969)

Kishlansky, Mark *The Rise of the New Model Army* (Cambridge, 1979)

Lindley, Keith *Fenland Riots and the English Revolution* (1982)

Lloyd, H.A. *The Gentry of South West Wales*

1540-1640 (Aberystwyth, Wales, 1968)

Lucas Philips, C.E. *Cromwell's Captains* (1938)

Manning, Brian *The English People and the English Revolution 1640-1649* (1976)

Marchant, R.A. *The Church Under the Law* (Cambridge, 1969)

Money, Walter *The First and Second Battles of Newbury and the Siege of Donnington Castle 1643-46* (1881)

Moody, T.W. *et al* (eds.) *The New History of Ireland, Volume 3, Early Modern Ireland 1534-1691* (Oxford, 1976)

Morrah, P. *Prince Rupert of the Rhine* (1976)

Morrill, John *Cheshire 1630-1660. County Government and Society during the 'English Revolution'* (Oxford, 1974)

—— *The Revolt of the Provinces. Conservatism and Radicalism in the English Civil War 1630-1650* rev. edn (1980)

—— (ed.) *Reactions to the English Civil War 1642-1649* (1982)

Newman, P.R. *Marston Moor 1644* (Chichester, 1981)

—— *Royalist Officers in England and Wales 1642-1660: A Biographical Dictionary* (New York, 1981)

Parry, R.H. (ed.) *The English Civil War and After 1642-58* (1970)

Phillips, John Rowland *Memorials of the Civil War in Wales and the Marches 1642-49*, 2 vols. (1874)

Rogers, H.C.B. *Battles and Generals of the Civil Wars 1642-51* (1968)

Rogers, P.G. *The Fifth Monarchy Men* (1966)

Roots, Ivan *The Great Rebellion 1642-60* (1966)

Russell, C. *The Crisis of Parliaments* (Oxford 1971)

—— (ed.) *The Origins of the English Civil War* (1973)

Schwoerer, L. *No Standing Armies! The Anti-Army Ideology in 17th Century England* (1974)

Sherwood, R.E. *Civil Strife in the Midlands* (Chichester, 1974)

Stevenson, D. *The Scottish Revolution 1637-1644* (London, n.d.)

Thirsk, J. (ed.) *The Agrarian History of England 1500-1640* (Cambridge, 1967)

Thomas, K.V. *Religion and the Decline of Magic* (1971)

Trevor-Roper, H.R. *Archbishop Laud* 2nd edn (1962)

Underdown, David *Royalist Conspiracy in England 1649-1660* (Yale, 1960)

—— *Pride's Purge* (1971)

—— *Somerset in the Civil War and Interregnum* (Newton Abbot, 1973)

Watkins, O.C. *The Puritan Experience* (1972)

Webb, J. *Memorials of the Civil War as it Affected Herefordshire and the Adjacent Counties* (1879)

Wedgwood, C.V. *The King's Peace* (1955)

—— *The King's War* (1958)

Wenham, L.P. *The Great and Close Siege of York 1644* (Kineton, 1970)

Wood, A.C. *Nottinghamshire in the Civil War* (Oxford, 1937)

Woolrych, Austin, *Battles of the English Civil War* (1961)

—— *Commonwealth to Protectorate* (Oxford, 1982)

Worden, B. *The Rump Parliament* (Cambridge, 1974)

Young, P. *Edgehill 1642 The Campaign and the Battle* (Kineton, 1967)

Young P. and Holmes, R. *The English Civil War: A Military History of the Three Civil Wars 1642-1651* (1974)

Young, P. and Toynbee, M. *Cropredy Bridge 1644. The Campaign and the Battle* (Kineton, 1970)

Zagorin, P. *The Court and the Country: The Beginning of the English Revolution* (1969)

INDEX

57, 71, 81, 83
Glencairn, earl of 111
Gloucester, city and garrison of 9,
  12, 31, 35, 37, 39, 51, 67, 73,
  81, 83, 87, 99
Gloucestershire, county of 21, 99,
  105
Goffe, Major General William 113
Gogar 101
Goring, George (Lord) 19, 25, 55,
  57, 59, 63, 67, 69, 71, 73, 75,
  77, 79, 81, 83
Grandison, Viscount 35
Grantham 29, 117
Great Trust, The 115
Greenhalgh Castle 71
Grenville, Sir Bevil 33
Grenville, Sir Richard 59
Grey of Groby, Lord 91
Guernsey, Island of 111
Guilsborough 73
Gunter, Colonel George 109

Haddington 101
Halifax 45
Hambledon 109
Hambledon Hill 79
Hamburg 57
Hamilton, marquess (dukes) of 17,
  89, 91, 99, 107
Hampden, John 31
Hampshire, County of 47, 61, 109
Hampton Court 85, 111
Handborough Bridge 51
Harlech Castle 83
Harrison, Major General Thomas
  97
Hartford Green 115
Hastings, Henry (Lord) 43, 73
Haverfordwest 37
Hawarden 37, 115
Haynes, Hezekiah 113
Heale 109
Helmsley Castle 53, 71
Henderson, Sir John 29
Henley on Thames 51
Henrietta Maria, Queen 25, 29, 39,
  51, 99
Heptonstall 45
Hereford, City and garrisons of 21,
  37, 75, 79, 81
Herefordshire, County of 79
Hertford, marquess of 19, 31, 33,
  37
Hertfordshire, County of 29
Hesilrige, Sir Arthur 35, 49
Hessay 55
Hexham 53
High Court of Justice, The 89, 95,
  111
Highnam, battle of 31, 37
Hilton, battle of 41
Hindon 109

Hinfield Moor, battle of 27
Hinton Ampner 49
Hobbal Grange 109
Holdenby House 84
Holland, earl of 89
Holt 81
Holt Castle 37
Holywell 37
Hopton Heath, battle of 31, 39
Hopton, Sir Ralph (Lord) 11, 12,
  19, 33, 35, 39, 47, 49, 51, 61,
  63, 65, 83
Hornby Castle 89
Horsebridge 59
Hotham, Captain John 25
Hotham, Sir John 25
Houghton, Sir Gilbert 27
Houghton Bridge 109
Houghton Common, battle of 27
Houghton Tower 27
Houlbourne, General 67
Hounslow 31
Hounslow Heath 85
Howard, Charles 113
Howley House 25
Huish Episcopi 77
Hull, port and garrisons of 11, 19,
  25, 29, 39, 41, 45, 47, 111
Humber, River 25
Humble Petition and Advice, The
  97
Hunslet 45
Huntingdon 81
Huntly, marquess of 17
Hursley 109
Hurst Castle 91
Hyde, Edward (earl of Clarendon)
  111

Ilchester 77
Inchiquin, Lord 93, 95
Independents, The 84, 91
Instrument of Government, The 97,
  113
Interregnum, The 95
Inverary 69
Inverkeithing 103
Inverlochy, battle of 69
Inverness 17, 99
Ireland 10, 35, 37, 43, 47, 51, 77,
  91, 93, 95, 97, 113, 115
Ireland, Gilbert 115
Ireton, Henry 75, 95
Irish Confederacy, The 51, 93, 95
'Irish' Troops 37, 43, 47, 51, 67,
  69, 83, 93
Isham 19
Isle of Ely 29
Isle of Man 105, 111
Isle of Wight 85, 91
Islip 51

Jermyn, Henry (Lord) 99

Jersey, Island of 99, 111
Jones, Michael 93, 95
Joyce, Cornet 85
Julianstown, battle of 93

Kelsey, Major General Thomas
  113
Kelsoe 17
Kennet, River 61
Kent, County of 7, 9, 87
Kentford Heath 85
Kilham 45
Kilkenny, 93, 95
Kilsyth, battle of 69
Kineton 21, 23
Kineton Heath 19
King, James (Lord Eythin) 57
Kingsclere 61
Kingston on Thames 89
Kinver, Forest of 9
Kinver Heath 109
Kirkham 27
Kirklees 45
Kislingbury 73
Knaresborough 71, 89
Knockanoss, battle of 93
Kyle of Sutherland 99

Laggan Army, The 93
Lambert, John 12, 45, 87, 97, 101,
  103, 105, 113, 115, 117
Lambourne, River 61, 63
Lancashire, County of 7, 9, 19, 27,
  37, 39, 45, 55, 57, 65, 71, 89,
  105, 115
Lancaster, town of 27
Lane, Colonel 109
Lane, Jane 109
Langdale, Sir Marmaduke 12, 41,
  71, 73, 75, 81, 87, 89, 111
Lango Green 27
Langport, battle of 77, 79, 81, 83
Lanhydrock 59
Lansdown Hill, battle of 12, 33, 39
Lathom House 27, 55, 71
Laugharne, Rowland 81, 87
Launceston 33, 59
Lea, River 29
Lea Hall 79
Ledbury 67
Lee Bridge, battle of 37
Leeds 25, 45, 55
Leicester, Forest of 9
Leicestershire, County of 67
Leigh, battle of 27
Leinster 93
Leintwardine 79
Leith 17, 101
Leslie, David 59, 69, 99, 101, 103,
  107
Levellers, The 91, 97, 111
Leven, earl of 41, 55, 69, 73, 81
Leveson, Thomas 43